THE
NATURE
— OF —
CALIFORNIA

AN INTRODUCTION TO FAMILIAR PLANTS, ANIMALS & OUTSTANDING NATURAL ATTRACTIONS

WATERFORD PRESS

Reviews for the 1st edition of *The Nature of California*:

"The Nature of California offers an agreeable overview of animals and plants casual hikers and campers are likely to encounter . . . a useful book to keep with the picnic supplies or camping gear."

Los Angeles Times

"With so many detailed guides in print, it would be tempting to overlook this book, yet it fills a valuable niche. Small and light, [it features] lovely color illustrations of several hundred species of plants, mammals, reptiles, fish and birds."

San Francisco Chronicle

"A useful and informative guide . . . this is a user-friendly book with an excellent introduction."

Books of the Southwest Review

"A colorful paperback field guide for people of all ages."

California Biodiversity News

THE
NATURE
— OF —
CALIFORNIA

AN INTRODUCTION TO FAMILIAR PLANTS, ANIMALS & OUTSTANDING NATURAL ATTRACTIONS

By James Kavanagh

Illustrations by Raymond Leung

Introduction by James C. Rettie

WATERFORD PRESS

Publisher's Cataloging in Publication Data
Kavanagh, James Daniel, 1960-
The Nature of California. An Introduction to Familiar Plants, Animals & Outstanding Natural Attractions (2nd ed). Includes bibliographical references and index.
1. Natural History – California. 2. Animals – Identification – California.
3. Plants – Identification – California. 4. Tourism – California.

Library of Congress Catalog Card Number: 2005936118
ISBN 10: 1-58355-301-0
ISBN 13: 978-1-58355-301-5

The introductory essay, "BUT A WATCH IN THE NIGHT" by JAMES C. RETTIE is from FOREVER THE LAND by RUSSELL AND KATE LORD. Copyright © 1950 by Harper & Brothers, copyright renewed © 1978 by Russell and Kate Lord. Reprinted with permission of HarperCollins Publishers.

The author would like to acknowledge the following individuals who assisted in the research and development of the first edition of this guide: William E. Grenfell Jr., H. William Lunt Ph.D, Ken McKowen, Judson Vandevere.

Waterford's toll-free order/information line is (800) 434-2555. Download hundreds of educational activities and games from our website: **www.waterfordpress.com**

While every attempt has been made to ensure the accuracy of the information in this guide, it is important to note that experts often disagree with one another regarding the common name, size, appearance, habitat, distribution and taxonomy of species. For permissions, or to share comments, e-mail editor@waterfordpress.com.

Printed in China

CONTENTS

To Jill

PREFACE

The Nature of California is intended to provide novice naturalists with a pocket reference to common and unusual species of plants and animals and the outstanding natural attractions found in California

The guide's primary purpose is to introduce the reader to familiar plants and animals and to highlight the diversity of species found in California. Its secondary purpose is to show how all species in each ecosystem found here depend on each other, directly and indirectly, for survival.

Environmental education begins when individuals learn to appreciate the plants and animals in their immediate environment. When they start to care about local species – which often begins by learning their names – they take the first step toward understanding their place (as an animal) within an ecosystem.

The guide opens with a brief introduction to evolution. This is not intended in any way to dispute creationism, but is merely intended to illustrate the similarities and differences between major groups of plants and animals and show when each appeared in geologic time. To study the fossil record is fascinating in and of itself, but one of the most stunning things it reveals is a number of transitional species that are intermediary between different classes of organisms.

The brilliant introductory essay by James C. Rettie provides a simplified view of the evolution of life on earth, and the role that man – the animal – has played to date.

I am indebted to dozens of helpful people who assisted me in the monumental task of researching and writing this guide, including staff at the California Department of Parks and Recreation, the California Department of Fish and Game, the U.S. Fish and Wildlife Service, the California Office of Tourism, the Boy Scouts and Girl Scouts of America and the California Academy of Sciences. I would like to thank my critics at these organizations and other experts who reviewed an early draft of the guide and contributed hundreds of valuable comments and criticisms.

J.D.K.

BUT A WATCH IN THE NIGHT

BY JAMES C. RETTIE

James C. Rettie wrote the following essay while working for the National Forest Service in 1948. In a flash of brilliance, he converted the statistics from an existing government pamphlet on soil erosion into an analogy for the ages.

OUT BEYOND OUR SOLAR SYSTEM there is a planet called Copernicus. It came into existence some four or five billion years before the birth of our earth. In due course of time it became inhabited by a race of intelligent men.

About 750 million years ago the Copernicans had developed the motion picture machine to a point well in advance of the stage that we have reached. Most of the cameras that we now use in motion picture work are geared to take twenty-four pictures per second on a continuous strip of film. When such film is run through a projector, it throws a series of images on the screen and these change with a rapidity that gives the visual impression of normal movement. If a motion is too swift for the human eye to see it in detail, it can be captured and artificially slowed down by means of the slow-motion camera. This one is geared to take many more shots per second – ninety-six or even more than that. When the slow motion film is projected at the normal speed of twenty-four pictures per second, we can see just how the jumping horse goes over a hurdle.

What about motion that is too slow to be seen by the human eye? That problem has been solved by the use of the time-lapse camera. In this one, the shutter is geared to take only one shot per second, or one per minute, or even one per hour – depending upon the kind of movement that is being photographed. When the time-lapse film is projected at the normal speed of twenty-four pictures per second, it is possible to see a bean sprout growing up out of the ground. Time-lapse films are useful in the study of many types of motion too slow to be observed by the unaided, human eye.

The Copernicans, it seems, had time-lapse cameras some 757 million years ago and they also had superpowered telescopes that gave them a clear view of what was happening upon this earth. They decided to make a film record of the life history of earth and to make it on the scale of one picture per year. The photography has been in progress during the last 757 million years.

In the near future, a Copernican interstellar expedition will arrive upon our earth and bring with it a copy of the time-lapse film. Arrangements will be made for showing the entire film in one continuous run. This will begin at midnight of New Year's eve and continue day and night without a single stop until midnight on December 31. The rate of projection will be 24 pictures per second. Time on the screen will thus seem to move at the rate of twenty-four years per second; 1440 years per minute; 86,400 years per hour; approximately two million years per day and sixty-two million years per month. The normal lifespan of individual man will occupy about three seconds. The full period of earth history that will be unfolded on the screen (some 757 million years) will extend from what the geologists call the Pre-Cambrian times up to the present. This will, by no means, cover the full time-span of the earth's geological history but it will embrace the period since the advent of living organisms.

During the months of January, February, and March the picture will be desolate and dreary. The shape of the land masses and the oceans will bear little or no resemblance to those that we know. The violence of geological erosion will be much in evidence. Rains will pour down on the land and promptly go booming down to the seas. There will be no clear streams anywhere except where the rains fall upon hard rock. Everywhere on the steeper ground the stream channels will be filled with boulders hurled down by rushing waters. Raging torrents and dry stream beds will keep alternating in quick succession. High mountains will seem to melt like so much butter in the sun. The shifting of land into the seas, later to be thrust up as new mountains, will be going on at a grand scale.

Early in April there will be some indication of the presence of single-celled living organisms in some of the warmer and sheltered coastal waters. By the end of the month it will be noticed that some of these organisms have become multicellular. A few of them, including the Trilobites, will be encased in hard shells.

Toward the end of May, the first vertebrates will appear, but they will still be aquatic creatures. In June about 60 percent of the land area that we know as North America will be under water. One broad channel will occupy the space where the Rocky Mountains now stand. Great deposits of limestone will be forming under some of the shallower seas. Oil and gas deposits will be in process of formation – also under shallow seas. On land there will be no sign of vegetation. Erosion will be rampant, tearing loose particles and chunks of rock and grinding them into sand and silt to be spewed out by the streams into bays and estuaries.

About the middle of July the first land plants will appear and take up the tremendous job of soil building. Slowly, very slowly, the mat of vegetation will spread, always battling for its life against the power of erosion. Almost foot by foot, the plant life will advance, lacing down with its root structures whatever pulverized rock material it can find. Leaves and stems will be giving added protection against the loss of the soil foothold. The increasing vegetation will pave the way for the land animals that will live upon it.

Early in August the seas will be teeming with fish. This will be what geologists call the Devonian period. Some of the races of these fish will be breathing by means of lung tissue instead of through gill tissues. Before the month is over, some of the lung fish will go ashore and take on a crude lizard-like appearance. Here are the first amphibians.

In early September the insects will put in their appearance. Some will look like huge dragonflies and will have a wing span of 24 inches. Large portions of the land masses will now be covered with heavy vegetation that will include the primitive spore-propagating trees. Layer upon layer of this plant growth will build up, later to appear as coal deposits. About the middle of this month, there will be evidence of the first seed-bearing plants and the first reptiles. Heretofore, the land animals will have been amphibians that could reproduce their kind only by depositing a soft egg mass in quiet waters. The reptiles will be shown to be freed from the aquatic bond because they can reproduce by means of a shelled egg in which the embryo and its nurturing liquids are sealed and thus protected from destructive evaporation. Before September is over, the first dinosaurs will be seen – creatures destined to dominate the animal realm for about 140 million years and then to disappear.

In October there will be series of mountain uplifts along what is now the eastern coast of the United States. A creature with feathered limbs – half bird and half reptile in appearance – will take itself into the air. Some small and rather unpretentious animals will be seen to bring forth their young in a form that is a miniature replica of the parents and to feed these young on milk secreted by mammary glands in the female parent. The emergence of this mammalian form of animal life will be recognized as one of the great events in geologic time. October will also witness the high-water mark of the dinosaurs – creatures ranging in size from that of the modern goat to monsters like Brontosaurus that weighed some 40 tons. Most of them will be placid vegetarians, but a few will be hideous-looking carnivores, like Allosaurus and Tyrannosaurus. Some of the herbivorous dinosaurs will be clad in bony armor for protection against their flesh-eating comrades.

November will bring pictures of a sea extending from the Gulf of Mexico to the Arctic in space now occupied by the Rocky Mountains. A few of the reptiles will take to the air on bat-like wings. One of these, called Pteranodon, will have a wingspread of 15 feet. There will be a rapid development of the modern flowering plants, modern trees, and modern insects. The dinosaurs will disappear. Toward the end of the month there will be a tremendous land disturbance in which the Rocky Mountains will rise out of the sea to assume a dominating place in the North American landscape.

INTRODUCTION

As the picture runs on into December it will show the mammals in command of the animal life. Seed-bearing trees and grasses will have covered most of the land with a heavy mantle of vegetation. Only the areas newly thrust up from the sea will be barren. Most of the streams will be crystal clear. The turmoil of geological erosion will be confined to localized areas. About December 25 will begin the cutting of the Grand Canyon of the Colorado River. Grinding down through layer after layer of sedimentary strata, this stream will finally expose deposits laid down in Pre-Cambrian times. Thus in the walls of that canyon will appear geological formations dating from recent times to the period when the earth had no living organisms upon it.

The picture will run on through the latter days of December and even up to its final day with still no sign of mankind. The spectators will become alarmed in the fear that man has somehow been left out. But not so; sometime about noon on December 31 (one million years ago) will appear a stooped, massive creature of man-like proportions. This will be Pithecanthropus, the Java ape man. For tools and weapons he will have nothing but crude stone and wooden clubs. His children will live a precarious existence threatened on the one side by hostile animals and on the other by tremendous climatic changes. Ice sheets – in places 4,000 feet deep – will form in the northern parts of North America and Eurasia. Four times this glacial ice will push southward to cover half the continents. With each advance the plant and animal life will be swept under or pushed southward. With each recession of the ice, life will struggle to re-establish itself in the wake of the retreating glaciers. The woolly mammoth, the musk ox, and the caribou all will fight to maintain themselves near the ice line. Sometimes they will be caught and put into cold storage – skin, flesh, blood, bones, and all.

The picture will run on through supper time with still very little evidence of man's presence on earth. It will be about 11 o'clock when Neanderthal man appears. Another half hour will go by before the appearance of Cro-Magnon man living in caves and painting crude animal pictures on the walls of his dwelling. Fifteen minutes more will bring Neolithic man, knowing how to chip stone and thus produce sharp cutting edges for spears and tools. In a few minutes more it will appear that man has domesticated the dog, the sheep and, possibly, other animals. He will then begin the use of milk. He will also learn the arts of basket weaving and the making of pottery and dugout canoes.

The dawn of civilization will not come until about five or six minutes before the end of the picture. The story of the Egyptians, the Babylonians, the Greeks, and the Romans will unroll during the fourth, the third, and the second minute before the end. At 58 minutes and 43 seconds past 11:00 P.M. (just 1 minute and 17 seconds before the end) will come the beginning of the Christian era. Columbus will discover the new world 20 seconds before the end.

The Declaration of Independence will be signed just 7 seconds before the final curtain comes down.

In those few moments of geologic time will be the story of all that has happened since we became a nation. And what a story it will be! A human swarm will sweep across the face of the continent and take it away from the [Native Americans]. They will change it far more radically than it has ever been changed before in a comparable time. The great virgin forests will be seen going down before ax and fire. The soil, covered for eons by its protective mantle of trees and grasses, will be laid bare to the ravages of water and wind erosion. Streams that had been flowing clear will, once again, take up a load of silt and push it toward the seas. Humus and mineral salts, both vital elements of productive soil, will be seen to vanish at a terrifying rate.

The railroads and highways and cities that will spring up may divert attention, but they cannot cover up the blight of man's recent activities. In great sections of Asia, it will be seen that man must utilize cow dung and every scrap of available straw or grass for fuel to cook his food. The forests that once provided wood for this purpose will be gone without a trace. The use of these agricultural wastes for fuel, in place of returning them to the land, will be leading to increasing soil impoverishment. Here and there will be seen a dust storm darkening the landscape over an area a thousand miles across. Man-creatures will be shown counting their wealth in terms of bits of printed paper representing other bits of a scarce but comparatively useless yellow metal that is kept buried in strong vaults. Meanwhile, the soil, the only real wealth that can keep mankind alive on the face of this earth is savagely being cut loose from its ancient moorings and washed into the seven seas.

We have just arrived upon this earth. How long will we stay?

HOW TO USE THIS BOOK

Because this guide has been written for the novice, every attempt has been made to simplify presentation of the material. Illustrations are accompanied by brief descriptions of key features, and technical terms have been held to a minimum. Plants and animals are arranged more-or-less in their taxonomic groupings. Exceptions have been made when nontraditional groupings facilitate field identification for the novice (e.g., wildflowers are grouped by color).

SPECIES DESCRIPTION

The species descriptions have been fragmented to simplify presentation of information:

① **CALIFORNIA QUAIL**
② *Callipepla californica*
③ **Size:** 9-11 in. (23-28 cm)
④ **Description:** Plump bird with blue chest, black face and forward-curving plume (teardrop topknot).
⑤ **Habitat:** Mixed woodlands, open brushy areas, suburban parks.
⑥ **Comments:** Flocks descend on city parks and gardens after breeding season to feed on seeds and invertebrates. California's state bird.

① **COMMON NAME**

The name in bold type indicates the common name of the species. It is important to note that a single species may have many common names.

② *Scientific Name*

The italicized latin words refer to an organism's scientific name, a universally accepted two-part term that precisely defines its relationship to other organisms. The first capitalized word, the genus, refers to groups of closely related organisms. The second term, the species name, refers to organisms that look similar and interbreed freely. If the second word in the term is 'spp.', this indicates there are several species in the genus that look similar to the one illustrated. If a third word appears in the term, it identifies a subspecies, a group of individuals that are even more closely related.

③ **Size**

Generally indicates the maximum length of animals (nose to tail tip) and the maximum height of plants. Exceptions are noted in the text.

④ **Description**
Refers to key markings and/or characteristics that help to distinguish a species.

⑤ **Habitat**
Where a species lives/can be found.

⑥ **Comments**
General information regarding distinctive behaviors, diet, vocalizations, related species, etc.

ILLUSTRATIONS

The majority of animal illustrations show the adult male in its breeding coloration. Plant illustrations are designed to highlight the characteristics that are most conspicuous in the field. It is important to note that illustrations are merely meant as guidelines; coloration, size and shape will vary depending on age, sex or season.

SPECIES CHECKLISTS

The species checklists at the back of this book are provided to allow you to keep track of the plants and animals you identify.

TIPS ON FIELD IDENTIFICATION

Identifying a species in the field can be as simple as one, two, three:

1. Note key markings, characteristics and/or behaviors;
2. Find an illustration that matches; and
3. Read the text to confirm your sighting.

Identifying mammals or birds in the field is not fundamentally different than identifying trees, flowers or other forms of life. It is simply a matter of knowing what to look for. Reading the introductory text to each section will make you aware of key characteristics of each group and allow you to use the guide more effectively in the field.

N.B. – *We refer primarily to familiar species in this guide and do not list all species within any group. References listed in the bibliography at the back of this guide provide more detailed information about specific areas of study.*

EVOLUTION OF ANIMALS

WHAT IS AN ANIMAL?

Animals are living organisms which can generally be distinguished from plants in four ways:
1) They feed on plants and other animals;
2) They have a nervous system;
3) They can move freely and are not rooted; and
4) Their cells do not have rigid walls or contain chlorophyll.

All animals are members of the animal kingdom, a group consisting of more than a million species. Species are classified within the animal kingdom according to their evolutionary relationships to one another.

Most of the animals discussed in this guide are members of the group called vertebrates. They all possess backbones and most have complex brains and highly developed senses.

The earliest vertebrates appeared in the oceans about 500 million years ago. Today, surviving species are divided into five main groups.

1. Fishes
2. Amphibians
3. Reptiles
4. Birds
5. Mammals

Following is a simplified description of the evolution of the vertebrates and the differences between groups.

FISHES

The oldest form of vertebrate life, fishes evolved from invertebrate sea creatures 400-500 million years ago. All are cold-blooded (ectothermic) and their activity levels are largely influenced by the surrounding environment.

The first species were armored and jawless and fed by filtering tiny organisms from water and mud. Surviving members of this group include lampreys and hagfishes. Jawless fishes were succeeded by jawed fishes that quickly came to dominate the seas, and still do today. The major surviving groups include:

1) **Sharks and rays** – more primitive species that possess soft skeletons made of cartilage; and

2) **Bony fishes** – a more advanced group of fishes that have bony skeletons, it includes most of the fishes currently existing.

Shark

Ray

Bony Fish

Physiological Characteristics of Fishes

Heart and gills

A two-chambered heart circulates the blood through a simple system of arteries and veins. Gills act like lungs and allow fishes to absorb dissolved oxygen from the water into their bloodstream.

Nervous system

Small anterior brain is connected to a spinal cord which runs the length of the body.

Digestive system

Digestive system is complete. A number of specialized organs produce enzymes which help to break down food in the stomach and intestines. Kidneys extract urine from the blood and waste is eliminated through the anus.

Reproduction

In most fishes, the female lays numerous eggs in water and the male fertilizes them externally. Young usually hatch as larvae, and the larval period ranges from a few hours to several years. Survival rate of young is low.

Senses

Most have the senses of taste, touch, smell, hearing and sight, although their vision is generally poor. Fishes hear and feel by sensing vibrations and temperature and pressure changes in the surrounding water.

AMPHIBIANS

The first limbed land-dwellers, amphibians evolved from fishes 300-400 million years ago and became the dominant land vertebrates for more than 100 million years. Like fishes, amphibians are cold-blooded and their activity levels are largely influenced by the environment.

The first fish-like amphibian ancestors to escape the water were those that had the ability to breathe air and possessed strong, paired fins that allowed them to wriggle onto mud-flats and sandbars. (Living relics of this group include five species of lungfish and the rare coelacanth.) Although amphibians were able to exploit rich new habitats on land, they remained largely dependent on aquatic environments for survival and reproduction.

The major surviving groups are:

1) **Salamanders** – slender-bodied, short-legged, long-tailed creatures that live secretive lives in dark, damp areas; and

2) **Frogs and toads** – squat-bodied animals with long hind legs, large heads and large eyes. Frogs are smooth skinned, toads have warty skin.

Salamander

Frog   Toad

Advances Made Over Fishes

Lungs and legs

By developing lungs and legs, amphibians freed themselves from the competition for food in aquatic environments and were able to flourish on land.

Improved circulatory system

Amphibians evolved a heart with three chambers that enhanced gas exchange in the lungs and provided body tissues with highly oxygenated blood.

Ears

Frogs and toads developed external ears that enhanced their hearing ability, an essential adaptation for surviving on land.

Reproduction

Most amphibians reproduced like fish. Salamanders differ in that most fertilize eggs internally rather than externally. In many, the male produced a sperm packet which the female collected and used to fertilize eggs as they were laid.

REPTILES

Reptiles appeared 300-350 million years ago. They soon came to dominate the earth, and continued to rule the land, sea and air for more than 130 million years. Cold-blooded like amphibians, reptiles evolved a host of characteristics that made them better suited for life on land.

About 65 million years ago, the dominant reptiles mysteriously underwent a mass extinction. A popular theory suggests this was caused by a giant meteor hitting the earth which sent up a huge dust cloud that blotted out the sun. The lack of sun and subsequently low temperatures caused many plants and animals to perish.

The major surviving reptilian groups are:

1) **Turtles** – hard-shelled reptiles with short legs;
2) **Lizards** – scaly-skinned reptiles with long legs and tails;
3) **Snakes** – long, legless reptiles with scaly skin; and
4) **Crocodilians** – very large reptiles with elongate snouts, toothy jaws and long tails.

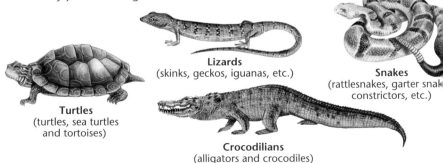

Lizards
(skinks, geckos, iguanas, etc.)

Snakes
(rattlesnakes, garter snakes, constrictors, etc.)

Turtles
(turtles, sea turtles and tortoises)

Crocodilians
(alligators and crocodiles)

Advances Made Over Amphibians

Dry, scaly skin
Their dry skin prevents water loss and also protects them from predators.

Posture
Many reptiles evolved an upright posture and strong legs which enhanced their mobility on land.

Improved heart and lungs
Their heart and lungs were more efficient which heightened their activity levels. The heart had four chambers – although the division between ventricles was usually incomplete – making it less likely that oxygenated and deoxygenated blood would mix.

Defense
They were agile and better able to defend themselves, having sharp claws and teeth or beaks capable of inflicting wounds.

BIRDS

Birds evolved from reptiles 100-200 million years ago. Unlike species before them, birds were warm-blooded (endothermic) and able to regulate their body temperature internally.* This meant that they could maintain high activity levels despite fluctuations in environmental temperature. They are believed to have evolved from a group of gliding reptiles, with their scaly legs considered proof of their reptilian heritage.

Birds come in a vast array of groups. All have feathered bodies, beaks, lack teeth and have forelimbs modified into wings. Most can fly.

Advances Made Over Reptiles

Ability to fly
By evolving flight, birds were able to exploit environments that were inaccessible to their competitors and predators. The characteristics they evolved that allowed them to fly included wings, feathers, hollow bones and an enhanced breathing capacity.

Warm-blooded
An insulating layer of feathers enhanced their capacity to retain heat. They also had true four-chambered hearts that enhanced their ability to maintain high activity levels in varying environments.

Keen senses
Birds evolved very keen senses of vision and hearing and developed complex behavioral and communicative patterns.

Reproduction
Fertilization was internal and the eggs had hard, rather than leathery, shells. Unlike most reptiles, birds incubated their eggs themselves and protected and nurtured their young for a period of time following birth.

* There is still a debate over whether or not some dinosaurs were warm-blooded.

MAMMALS

Mammals evolved from reptiles 100-200 million years ago. Though warm-blooded like birds, they are believed to have different reptilian ancestors. In addition to being warm-blooded, mammals also evolved physiological adaptations which allowed them to hunt prey and avoid predation better than their competitors.

Mammals quickly exploited the habitats left vacant by the dinosaurs and have been the dominant land vertebrates for the past 65 million years. Man is a relatively new addition to the group, having a lineage of less than 3 million years.

Mammals have evolved into three distinct groups, all of which have living representatives:

1) **Monotremes** – egg-laying mammals;
2) **Marsupials** – pouched mammals which bear living, embryonic young; and
3) **Placentals** – mammals which bear fully-developed young.

Monotremes
(platypus and echidna)

Marsupials
(opossums,
kangaroos etc.)

Placentals
(squirrels, humans,
dogs, rats etc.)

Advances Made Over Birds

Reproduction
Fertilization was internal, but in most, the young developed in the female's uterus instead of an egg. After birth, the young were fed and nurtured by adults for an extensive period, during which they learned behavioral lessons from their elders and siblings. This emphasis on learned responses at an early age is believed to contributed to the superior intelligence and reproductive success of the group.

Hearing
Most had three bones in the middle ear to enhance hearing. (Birds and reptiles have one.)

Teeth
Many developed specialized teeth that allowed them to rely on a variety of food sources. Incisors were for cutting, canines for tearing and molars for chewing or shearing.

Breathing
Mammals evolved a diaphragm which increased breathing efficiency.

Posture
Many evolved long, strong legs and were very agile on land.

EVOLUTION OF PLANTS

WHAT IS A PLANT?

Plants are living organisms which can generally be distinguished from animals in four ways:

1) They synthesize their own food needed for maintenance and growth from carbon dioxide, water and sunlight;
2) They do not have a nervous system;
3) Most are rooted and cannot move around easily; and
4) Their cells have rigid walls and contain chlorophyll, a pigment needed for photosynthesis.

All plants are members of the plant kingdom. According to the fossil record, plants evolved from algae that originated nearly 3 billion years ago. Since then, plants have evolved into millions of species in a mind-boggling assortment of groups.

Most North American plants are classified into two main groups:

1) **Gymnosperms** – plants with naked seeds; and
2) **Angiosperms** – flowering plants with enclosed seeds.

Gymnosperms   Angiosperms

GYMNOSPERMS – THE NAKED SEED PLANTS

This group of mostly evergreen trees and shrubs includes some of the largest and oldest known plants. They began to appear around 300-400 million years ago, and were the dominant plant species on earth for nearly 200 million years. The most successful surviving group of gymnosperms are the conifers, which include such species as pines, spruces, firs, larches and junipers.

Most conifers are evergreen and have small needle-like or scale-like leaves which are adapted to withstand extreme temperature changes. Some species are deciduous, but most retain their leaves for two or more years before shedding them.

Reproduction

Most conifers produce cones – wood-like fruits that contain the male and female gametes. The male cones produce pollen that is carried by the wind to settle between the scales of female cones on other trees. The pollen stimulates ovules to change into seeds, and the scales of the female cone close up to protect the seeds. When the seeds are ripe, up to two years later, environmental conditions stimulate the cone to open its scales and the naked seeds to fall to the ground.

ANGIOSPERMS – THE FLOWERING PLANTS

Angiosperms first appeared in the fossil record around 130 million years ago. They quickly adapted to a wide variety of environments and succeeded gymnosperms as the dominant land plants. Their reproductive success was largely due to two key adaptations:

Advances Made Over Gymnosperms

1) They produced flowers which attracted pollinating agents such as insects and birds; and
2) They produced seeds encased in fruits to aid in seed dispersal.

Angiosperms are classified in two main groups:

1) Monocots – plants with one embryonic leaf at germination, parallel-veined leaves, stems with scattered vascular bundles with little or no cambium (group includes grasses, cattails, orchids and corn); and

2) Dicots – plants with two embryonic leaves at germination, net-veined leaves, stems with cylindrical vascular bundles in a regular pattern that contain cambium (group includes more than 200,000 species ranging from tiny herbs to huge trees).

Angiosperms make up a diverse and widespread group of plants ranging from trees and shrubs such as oaks, cherries, maples, hazelnuts and apples, to typical flowers like lilies, orchids, roses, daisies, and violets. The trees and shrubs within this group are commonly referred to as deciduous and most shed their leaves annually.

Reproduction

A typical flower has colorful petals that encircle the male and female reproductive structures (see illustration p. 121). The male stamens are composed of thin filaments supporting anthers containing pollen. The female pistil contains unfertilized seeds in the swollen basal part called the ovary. Pollination occurs when pollen, carried by the wind or animals, reaches the pistil.

Once fertilization has occurred, the ovules develop into seeds and the ovary into a fruit. The fruit and seeds mature together, with the fruit ripening to the point where the seeds are capable of germinating. At maturity, each seed contains an embryo and a food supply to nourish it upon germination. Upon ripening, the fruit may fall to the ground with the seeds still inside, as in peaches, cherries and squash, or it may burst open and scatter its seeds in the wind, like poplar trees, willows and dandelions.

Fruit comes in many forms, from grapes, tomatoes, apples and pears, to pea and bean pods, nuts, burrs and capsules. Regardless of its shape, fruit enhances the reproductive success of angiosperms in two important ways. First, it helps to protect the seeds from the elements until they have fully matured, enabling them to survive unfavorable conditions. Secondly, fruit aids in seed dispersal. Some fruits are eaten by animals that eventually release the seeds in their feces, an ideal growing medium. Others may be spiny or burred so they catch on the coats of animals, or may have special features which enable them to be carried away from their parent plant by the wind or water.

GEOLOGICAL TIMESCALE

ERA	PERIOD	MYA*	EVENTS
CENOZOIC	HOLOCENE	.01	Dominance of man.
CENOZOIC	QUATERNARY	2.5	First human civilizations.
CENOZOIC	TERTIARY	65	Mammals, birds, insects and angiosperms dominate the land.
MESOZOIC	CRETACEOUS	135	Dinosaurs extinct. Mammals, insects and angiosperms undergo great expansion. Gymnosperms decline.
MESOZOIC	JURASSIC	190	Age of Reptiles; dinosaurs dominant. First birds appear.
MESOZOIC	TRIASSIC	225	First dinosaurs and mammals appear. Gymnosperms are dominant plants.
PALEOZOIC	PERMIAN	280	Great expansion of reptiles causes amphibians to decline. Many marine invertebrates become extinct.
PALEOZOIC	CARBONIFEROUS	340	Age of Amphibians; amphibians dominant. First reptiles appear. Fishes undergo a great expansion.
PALEOZOIC	DEVONIAN	400	Age of Fishes; fishes dominant. First amphibians, insects and gymnosperms appear.
PALEOZOIC	SILURIAN	430	First jawed fishes appear. Plants move onto land.
PALEOZOIC	ORDOVICIAN	500	First vertebrates appear.
PALEOZOIC	CAMBRIAN	600	Marine invertebrates and algae abundant.

*Millions of years ago

WHAT ARE MAMMALS?

Most mammals are warm-blooded, furred creatures that have 4 limbs and a tail, 5 digits on each foot, and several different kinds of teeth. All North American species give birth to live young which feed on milk from their mother's mammary glands.

HOW TO IDENTIFY MAMMALS

Mammals are generally secretive in their habits and therefore difficult to spot in the field. The best time to look for mammals is at dusk, dawn and at night, since many retreat to burrows during the day to escape the heat. Some of the best places to look for them are in undisturbed areas affording some source of cover such as wood edges and scrub thickets.

When you spot a mammal, consider its size, shape and color. Check for distinguishing field marks and note the surrounding habitat.

COMMON TRACKS

Studying tracks is an easy way to discover the kinds of mammals found in your area. For more information on animal tracks, see the references under mammals in the back of the guide.

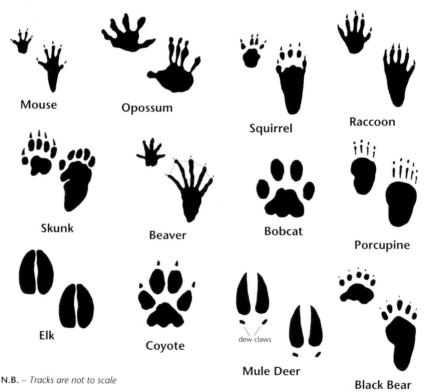

Mouse

Opossum

Squirrel

Raccoon

Skunk

Beaver

Bobcat

Porcupine

Elk

Coyote

Mule Deer

dew claws

Black Bear

N.B. – *Tracks are not to scale*

MARSUPIALS

Related to kangaroos and koalas, the opossum is the only marsupial found in North America. Young are born prematurely and move to a fur-lined pouch (marsupium) where they complete their development attached to a teat.

VIRGINIA OPOSSUM
Didelphis virginiana
Size: 25-40 in. (63-100 cm)
Description: Grayish fur, white face, black-tipped ears and naked, rat-like tail.
Habitat: Woodlands, farming areas, forest edges, suburban areas.
Comments: Most active in the evening and at night. It has the peculiar habit of pretending to be dead (playing possum) when frightened. An introduced species now widespread in California.

INSECTIVORES

Insectivores are generally small mammals with long snouts, short legs and sharp teeth. They live on or under the ground and feed on insects and other invertebrates.

ORNATE SHREW
Sorex ornatus
Size: 3-4 in. (8-10 cm)
Description: Gray-brown, mouse-like mammal with a pointed nose.
Habitat: Forests, wet meadows, chaparral forests, grasslands.
Comments: Shrews are exceedingly active and dart about under leaf litter and fallen logs on tiny runways. They have a very high metabolic rate and eat up to twice their own weight in food each day. Eleven species of shrew are found in California.

CALIFORNIA MOLE
Scapanus latimanus
Size: 5-8 in. (13-20 cm)
Description: Dark brown or gray fur; short hairy tail. Front feet broader than they are long.
Habitat: Moist soils.
Comments: Rarely seen above ground, their presence can be detected by the mounds of dirt they push up when tunneling. Four mole species are found in California.

BATS

The only true flying mammals, bats have large ears, small eyes and broad wings. Primarily nocturnal, they have developed a sophisticated sonar system – echolocation – to help them hunt insects at night. As they fly, they emit a series of high frequency sounds that bounce off objects and tell them what lies in their path. During daylight, they seek refuge in caves, trees and attics. Rarely harmful, bats are valuable in helping check insect populations. Twenty-three species occur in California.

BRAZILIAN FREE-TAILED BAT
Tadarida brasiliensis
Size: 4-5 in. (10-13 cm)
Description: Small chocolate-brown bat with velvety fur and a tail extending beyond the wing membrane.
Habitat: Roosts in caves and buildings.
Comments: Typically lives in large colonies of several thousand individuals.

CALIFORNIA MYOTIS
Myotis californicus
Size: 2-4 in. (5-10 cm)
Description: Distinguished by its small size. Coat is buff to brown with the hair bases much darker-colored than the tips.
Habitat: Crevices in caves, buildings, deserts, rocky areas.
Comments: Occurs in small colonies or singly. Often hawks for insects near the lower branches of trees. Flight is very erratic.

WESTERN RED BAT
Lasiurus blossevillii
Size: 3-5 in. (8-13 cm)
Description: Male is distinguished by its orange-red coat. Females are a duller red. Both sexes have a frosted breast.
Habitat: Forests.
Comments: Roosts in trees among heavy foliage that provides shade and cover during the day. Feeds at night on insects.

RABBITS & ALLIES

Members of this distinctive group of mammals have long ears, large eyes and long hind legs. Primarily nocturnal, they commonly rest in protected areas like thickets during the day. When threatened, they thump their hind feet on the ground as an alarm signal. Eight species occur in California.

BRUSH RABBIT
Sylvilagus bachmani
Size: 12-15 in. (30-38 cm)
Description: Small, brownish rabbit with short ears and a small tail.
Habitat: Thick brushy areas, chaparral.
Comments: Often spotted feeding at dusk and dawn. Young are active during the day.

BLACK-TAILED JACKRABBIT
Lepus californicus
Size: 20-25 in. (50-63 cm)
Description: Large gray or tan rabbit with long black-tipped ears and a black-streaked tail.
Habitat: Prairies and open areas.
Comments: Very athletic, they hop up to 10 feet (3 m) at a time and can reach speeds of 35 mph (56 kph). Active in late afternoon and evening.

DESERT COTTONTAIL
Sylvilagus audubonii
Size: 14-17 in. (35-43 cm)
Description: Larger than the brush rabbit with longer hind legs, medium-sized ears and a large white tail.
Habitat: Dry grasslands, open plains and deserts.
Comments: Feeds on a range of plants including grasses, mesquite and cactus. Uses stumps and sloping trees as lookouts.

SQUIRRELS & ALLIES

This diverse family of hairy-tailed, large-eyed rodents includes chipmunks, tree squirrels, ground squirrels and marmots. All but the tree squirrels live in burrows on or under the ground throughout the year. Most are active during the day and easily observed in the field. Size includes tail length.

MERRIAM'S CHIPMUNK
Tamias merriami
Size: 7-11 in. (18-28 cm)
Description: Small, gray-brown squirrel with indistinct side and face stripes.
Habitat: Mixed forests, brushland, chaparral.
Comments: Active during the day, it is very vocal and often heard twittering and chattering. Feeds mostly on seeds. The similar lodgepole chipmunk (*Tomias speciosus*) found at higher elevations has more distinct stripes.

WESTERN GRAY SQUIRREL
Sciurus griseus
Size: 17-23 in. (43-58 cm)
Description: Has a gray coat, light belly and bushy tail.
Habitat: Forested areas.
Comments: Lives in large leaf nests, usually high in trees. Active during the morning, it feeds on conifer seeds and acorns.

NORTHERN FLYING SQUIRREL
Glaucomys sabrinus
Size: 10-15 in. (25-38 cm)
Description: Distinguished by its gray-brown coat, whitish undersides and loose fold of skin between its front and hind legs.
Habitat: Mixed and coniferous forests.
Comments: By spread-eagling and stretching its flight skin taut, it glides between trees for distances that can exceed 150 ft. (46 m). It is the only nocturnal squirrel in the Pacific states.

CALIFORNIA GROUND SQUIRREL
Spermophilus beecheyi
Size: 14-20 in. (35-50 cm)
Description: Coat is brown-to-gray with white wash on neck and sides and a dark band down its back.
Habitat: Grasslands and open areas with low vegetation.
Comments: These ground-dwelling rodents are easily observed feeding in open areas and running in and out of their multi-chambered tunnels.

GOLDEN-MANTLED GROUND SQUIRREL
Spermophilus lateralis
Size: 9-12 in. (23-30 cm)
Description: Told by its coppery head and shoulders and long white side stripe bordered in black. Unlike similar-looking chipmunks, it lacks facial stripes.
Habitat: Moist coniferous forests in the mountains.
Comments: When predators approach, individuals will sound warning calls causing all to flee to the safety of their burrows. Those found near campgrounds are often very tame.

YELLOW-BELLIED MARMOT
Marmota flaviventris
Size: 18-28 in. (45-70 cm)
Description: Large, yellow-brown rodent with a yellow belly. Many have a white patch between the eyes.
Habitat: Rocky alpine areas to elevations of 12,000 ft. (3,650 m).
Comments: Primarily diurnal, it is conspicuous in the Sierras. Warning call is a repetitive, highly-pitched chirp.

BEAVER

Found on rivers, lakes and marshes, beavers are the largest North American rodents. Highly aquatic, they have webbed feet and long, broad tails which they slap on the water's surface when alarmed.

AMERICAN BEAVER
Castor canadensis
Size: 40-48 in. (1-1.2 m)
Description: Glossy brown coat, flat, scaly tail.
Habitat: Lakes, ponds and streams.
Comments: Many beavers live in dens excavated along banks; others build cone-shaped houses (lodges) of sticks and mud. Diet consists of the bark of deciduous trees and shrubs, including aspens, willows and maples.

MICE & ALLIES

Most members of this large group have large ears, long tails and breed throughout the year. Dedicated omnivores, they have adapted to practically every North American habitat.

WESTERN JUMPING MOUSE
Zapus princeps
Size: 8-10 in. (20-25 cm)
Description: Coat is olive above, yellowish on the sides and white below. Large hind legs and long tail assist it in bounding across the ground.
Habitat: Found in mountain meadows and open woodlands near water.
Comments: Capable of leaping up to 6 ft. (1.8 m).

DUSKY-FOOTED WOODRAT
Neotoma fuscipes
Size: 12-19 in. (30-48 cm)
Description: Large gray-brown rat with light underparts and a hairy tail.
Habitat: Chaparral, mixed forests, Sierra foothills.
Comments: Often builds large, cone-shaped stick houses that are conspicuous near trails.

CALIFORNIA VOLE
Microtus californicus
Size: 6-8 in. (15-20 cm)
Description: Brown-black mouse-sized mammal with pale feet and a short, bicolored tail.
Habitat: Forests, swamps and grassy meadows.
Comments: Eats grass, roots and seeds. Presence can be detected by the small tunnels they create under grass and snow.

BLACK RAT
Rattus rattus
Size: To 18 in. (45 cm)
Description: Black or brownish rodent with a long scaly tail.
Habitat: Dumps, buildings, waste areas.
Comments: Like the house mouse, this species was inadvertently introduced from Europe and is now widespread in North America. Often nests in trees and attics, which earned it it's other name, the roof rat. Its brownish cousin, the Norway rat (*R. norvegicus*) is also common in California.

Black Rat

Norway Rat

DEER MOUSE
Peromyscus maniculatus
Size: 4-9 in. (10-23 cm)
Description: Bicolored coat is pale gray to red-brown above and white below. Long, hairy tail is also bicolored.
Habitat: Common and widespread in a variety of habitats.
Comments: Feeds on seeds, buds, fruit and wild plants. Active year-round.

HOUSE MOUSE
Mus musculus
Size: 5-8 in. (13-20 cm)
Description: Told by its gray coat, large eyes and ears and scaly tail.
Habitat: Very common near human dwellings.
Comments: Normally lives in colonies. Females have up to 5 litters of 4-8 young annually.

PORCUPINES

Porcupines are medium-sized mammals with coats of stiff, barbed quills. When threatened, they face away from their aggressor, erect the quills and lash out with their tail. The loosely rooted quills detach on contact and are extremely difficult to remove.

COMMON PORCUPINE
Erethizon dorsatum
Size: 25-37 in. (63-93 cm)
Description: Chunky profile, arched back and long gray coat of barbed quills.
Habitat: Common in forests and shrubby ravines.
Comments: Feeds on leaves, twigs and bark and spends much of its time in trees.

RACCOONS & ALLIES

All members of this diverse family of dog-sized mammals have ringed tails.

COMMON RACCOON
Procyon lotor
Size: 25-37 in. (63-93 cm)
Description: Gray-brown coat, black mask and ringed tail.
Habitat: Wooded areas near water throughout California.
Comments: Feeds on small animals, insects, plants and refuse. It often dunks its food into water before eating it. Primarily nocturnal.

RINGTAIL
Bassariscus astutus
Size: 24-32 in. (60-80 cm)
Description: Has large eyes, large ears and a long ringed tail. Lacks a black mask.
Habitat: Rocky areas, rough country, chaparral.
Comments: Hunts at night, killing prey with a bite to the neck. Nicknamed 'Miners' Cats,' they were once used like cats to control rodent populations in mines.

WEASELS & ALLIES

Members of this group usually have small heads, long necks, short legs and long bodies. All but sea otters have prominent anal scent glands which are used for social and sexual communication.

AMERICAN BADGER
Taxidea taxus
Size: 20-34 in. (50-85 cm)
Description: A squat, heavy-bodied animal with a long, yellow-gray coat, white forehead stripe and long foreclaws.
Habitat: Grasslands and uncultivated pastures.
Comments: A prodigious digger, it feeds mostly on ground squirrels and other burrowing mammals.

STRIPED SKUNK
Mephitis mephitis
Size: 20-31 in. (50-78 cm)
Description: Black mammal with thin white forehead stripe and two white back stripes.
Habitat: Open wooded areas, farmland, suburbs.
Comments: Protects itself by spraying aggressors with noxious-smelling musk from its anal glands. Spray effective to 20 ft. (6 m) away. Feeds on vegetation, insects and small mammals.

WESTERN SPOTTED SKUNK
Spilogale gracilis
Size: 9-19 in. (23-48 cm)
Description: Black coat has 4-6 irregular stripes. White spots on head and sides.
Habitat: Mixed woodlands, wastelands.
Comments: When threatened, it gives warning by raising its tail, doing a handstand and spreading its hind feet before spraying. A good climber and swimmer, it is more agile than larger skunks.

NORTHERN RIVER OTTER
Lontra canadensis
Size: 40-52 in. (1-1.3 m)
Description: Sleek, long-bodied mammal has a glossy, gray-brown coat, thick tail and webbed hind feet.
Habitat: Found in lakes and rivers in northern California.
Comments: Hunts on land and in fresh and saltwater where it feeds on fishes, amphibians, crustaceans and small mammals. Fond of play, they often make slides along riverbanks in mud or snow.

LONG-TAILED WEASEL
Mustela frenata
Size: 13-22 in. (33-55 cm)
Description: Told by slender body and long, black-tipped tail. Summer coat is brown above, white below with brown feet. Above 4,000 ft. (1,220 m) the winter coat is all white except for black tip on tail.
Habitat: Found near water in open woodlands, meadows and fields.
Comments: Weasels are aggressive hunters and are notorious for killing more prey than they can eat.

SEA OTTER
Enhydra lutris
Size: 30-72 in. (75-180 cm)
Description: Long-bodied, glossy brown mammal with short legs, webbed feet and a thick tail. Face is yellowish.
Habitat: Kelp beds.
Comments: Feeds floating on its back and often uses a stone to break open shellfish and sea urchins.

MINK
Mustela vison
Size: 20-28 in. (50-70 cm)
Description: Told by rich brown coat; usually has white spotting on chin and throat.
Habitat: Common near water in a variety of habitats.
Comments: Highly aquatic, they den along river and stream banks and feed on fish, amphibians, crustaceans and small mammals.

DOG-LIKE MAMMALS

Members of this family have long snouts, erect ears and resemble domestic dogs in looks and habit. All are active year-round.

COMMON GRAY FOX
Urocyon cinereoargenteus
Size: 30-44 in. (75-110 cm)
Description: Distinguished by its coat that is blackish-gray above and rusty-white below.
Habitat: Wooded lowlands, swamps, chaparral.
Comments: A secretive, nocturnal species, it sometimes forages during the day. An excellent climber, it often seeks refuge in trees.

COYOTE
Canis latrans
Size: 40-52 in. (1-1.3 m)
Description: Yellow-gray dog with a pointed nose, rust legs and ears and a bushy, black-tipped tail.
Habitat: Wooded and open areas.
Comments: Largely a nocturnal hunter, it is often seen loping across fields at dawn and dusk. Holds tail down when running. Feeds on rodents, rabbits, berries and carrion.

CAT-LIKE MAMMALS

These highly specialized carnivores are renowned hunters. All have short faces, keen vision, powerful bodies and retractable claws. Most are nocturnal hunters.

MOUNTAIN LION
Felis concolor
Size: 6-9 ft. (1.8-2.7 m)
Description: Large tan cat has a whitish belly and long, black-tipped tail.
Habitat: Forests and chaparral in the mountains and foothills.
Comments: A solitary hunter, it feeds largely on cloven-hoofed mammals, hares and other small mammals. Also called cougar and puma.

BOBCAT
Lynx rufus
Size: 3-4 ft. (.9-1.2 m)
Description: Told by its spotted red-brown coat and short, black-striped tail.
Habitat: Scrubby open woodlands, thickets, marshes.
Comments: Named for its bobbed tail, it rests in thickets by day and hunts rabbits and rodents by night. Has a variety of calls similar to a domestic cat.

BEARS

This group includes the largest terrestrial carnivores in the world. All are heavy-bodied, large-headed animals, with short ears and small tails. Their sense of smell is keen, although their eyesight is generally poor.

BLACK BEAR
Ursus americanus
Size: 4-6 ft. (1.2-1.8 m)
Description: Coat is normally black, but cinnamon and blue-gray variants also occur.
Habitat: Primarily mountainous areas.
Comments: Diet is 85% vegetarian and consists of berries, vegetation, fish, insects, mammals and refuse. It scavenges much of the meat it eats.

HOOFED MAMMALS

This general grouping includes members of the deer and sheep families.

MULE DEER
Odocoileus hemionus
Size: 4-7.5 ft. (1.2-2.3 m)
Description: Distinguished by tan coat, large 'mule-sized' ears and black-tipped tail.
Habitat: Open forests and wooded river valleys, chaparral.
Comments: Essentially a solitary species, mule deer often form herds during mating season and winter. They feed mostly on shrubs, twigs and grasses. Males shed antlers January-March.

ELK
Cervus elaphus
Size: 6-9 ft. (1.8-2.7 m)
Description: Large deer with shaggy brown neck and light rump patch.
Habitat: Mountain meadows and open forests.
Comments: Subspecies of elk including tule elk and Roosevelt elk are protected on a number of reserves in California. Males shed antlers annually.

BIGHORN SHEEP
Ovis canadensis
Size: 5-6 ft. (1.5-1.8 m)
Description: Told by large coiled horns and white rump patch.
Habitat: Meadows in the mountains and foothills near rugged slopes.
Comments: Powerful climbers, they have specialized 'suction-cup' hooves which enhance their traction on rocky slopes. Males and females form separate herds for most of the year. Horns are never shed.

MARINE MAMMALS

This group includes a variety of mammals that live in the water. Sea lions and seals are carnivores that spend the majority of their time at sea, but come ashore to breed. The fish-like dolphins and whales spend all their time in the water, breathing air through blowholes set high on their heads. Unlike fish, finned marine mammals have horizontal, rather than vertical, tail flukes.

CALIFORNIA SEA LION
Zalophus californianus
Size: 5-8 ft. (1.5-2.4 m)
Description: Coat is brown when dry, black when wet. Males have high foreheads and are much larger than females.
Habitat: Found along sandy and rocky shorelines in colonies.
Comments: Males are very vocal, continually honking at one another when defending their territory. Diet consists of fish and squid. A famous resident pod lives at Fisherman's Wharf in San Francisco.

HARBOR SEAL
Phoca vitulina
Size: 4-6 ft. (1.2-1.8 m)
Description: Has a dark-spotted, yellow-brown coat.
Habitat: Coastal waters, harbors, bays.
Comments: Found basking along shorelines at all times of the day, often in large groups. Much less vocal than sea lion. Also called leopard seal.

NORTHERN ELEPHANT SEAL
Mirounga angustirostris
Size: To 13 ft. (3.9 m)
Description: Huge brown seals. Adult males have a large, overhanging snout and weigh up to 8,000 lbs. (3,628 kg).
Habitat: Sandy beaches from central to southern California.
Comments: Bulls battle each other for females and breeding territories from December to March.

PACIFIC WHITE-SIDED DOLPHIN
Lagenorhynchus obliquidens
Size: 6-8 ft. (1.8-2.4 m)
Description: Told by green-black body, pale side stripes and white belly.
Habitat: Spotted near shorelines in winter and spring.
Comments: Travels in large groups of up to 1,000 members. Feeds primarily on small fish and squid.

COMMON DOLPHIN
Delphinus delphis
Size: 6-9 ft. (1.8-2.7 m)
Description: Distinguished by its dark flippers, yellowish flanks and white belly.
Habitat: Deep and nearshore waters.
Comments: Travels in large schools and often follows ships.

DALL'S PORPOISE
Phocoenoides dalli
Size: 5-7 ft. (1.5-2.1 m)
Description: Told by black body and large white belly patch.
Habitat: Common in coastal waters, especially in winter.
Comments: Found in groups of 2 to 20 individuals. Often plays around ships. Porpoises are generally distinguished from dolphins by their shorter snouts and stockier bodies.

HUMPBACK WHALE
Megaptera novaeangliae
Size: 40-50 ft. (12-15 m)
Description: Dark whale has a humped back and very long flippers with scalloped edges. Underside of flippers and tail flukes is white.
Habitat: Coastal during migration.
Comments: Feeds primarily on small schooling fish like herring. One of the most vocal of whales, its haunting calls can be heard on the surface during calm days.

California's State Marine Mammal

GRAY WHALE
Eschrichtius robustus
Size: 36-50 ft. (10-15 m)
Description: Large, mottled, gray-blue whale has a small dorsal hump and 2-5 throat grooves. Skin is often blotched with abrasions, scars and parasitic barnacles which cluster on its head and back.
Habitat: Abundant in coastal waters during winter-spring migration.
Comments: Breeds in waters off Baja California. Feeds primarily on small schooling fish like herring.

FINBACK WHALE
Balaenoptera physalus
Size: 60-80 ft. (18-24 m)
Description: Large, flat-headed gray whale with light belly and posterior dorsal fin. Back has a prominent ridge between the dorsal fin and tail.
Habitat: Found nearshore and offshore throughout the year.
Comments: A baleen whale, it has a sieve-like structure in its mouth that is used to strain small crustaceans, fish and plankton from the water.

KILLER WHALE
Orcinus orca
Size: 15-30 ft. (4.5-9 m)
Description: Told by jet-black body, white belly and white eye spots.
Habitat: Offshore waters.
Comments: Known as 'sea wolves,' killer whales travel in groups of up to 40 individuals and hunt as a pack when attacking large whales. They are opportunistic carnivores and will feed on virtually any large marine animal. They have even been observed snatching seals and sea lions from shore. A member of the dolphin family, it is called a whale because of its large size.

WHAT ARE BIRDS?

Birds are warm-blooded, feathered animals with two wings and two legs. The majority can fly and those that cannot are believed to be descended from ancestors that did. Adaptations for flight include hollow bones and an enhanced breathing capacity. Birds also have an efficient four-chambered heart and are insulated against the weather to enhance temperature regulation.

HOW TO IDENTIFY BIRDS

As with other species, the best way to become good at identifying birds is simply to practice. The more birds you attempt to identify, the better you will become at distinguishing species.

When birding, the first thing to note is the habitat you are exploring, in order to know what kinds of birds to expect. When you spot a bird, check for obvious field marks. Note the shape of its silhouette and beak. Note the color and pattern of its feathers for distinguishing markings at rest and in flight. Is it small (sparrow), medium (crow), or large (heron)? Does it have any unusual behavioral characteristics?

If you are interested in enhancing your field skills, it is essential to become familiar with bird songs since many species that are difficult to observe in the field are readily identified by their distinctive song. Bird song tapes and CDs are available from nature stores and libraries.

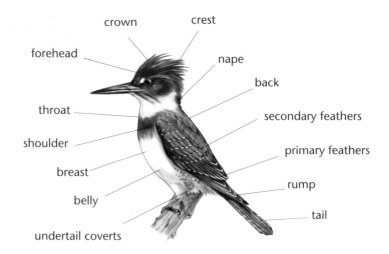

N.B. – *It is important to note that most species illustrations feature the adult male in its breeding coloration. Colors and markings shown may be duller or absent during different times of the year.*

GREBES

The members of this group of duck-like birds have short tails, slender necks and stiff bills. Excellent divers, they have lobed toes rather than webbed feet and have legs located near the back of the body to help propel them through the water.

PIED-BILLED GREBE
Podilymbus podiceps
Size: 12-15 in. (30-38 cm)
Description: Distinguished by its small size and chicken-like white bill. Breeding birds have a black-banded bill and black throat. Non-breeding adults are grayish.
Habitat: Freshwater ponds, lakes and weed-choked marshes.
Comments: Often swims with body partially submerged. Hatchlings are often carried and fed on the backs of their parents.

WESTERN GREBE
Aechmophorus occidentalis
Size: 20-29 in. (50-73 cm)
Description: Long-necked, slender-billed bird is black above, white below.
Habitat: Large lakes and coastal waters.
Comments: Winters along the coast in large numbers. Noted for their spectacular courtship display in which males and females run across the water's surface in pairs.

PELICANS & ALLIES

These web-footed birds are common along coastlines and inland lakes.

BROWN PELICAN
Pelecanus occidentalis
Size: 3-5 ft. (.9-1.5 m)
Description: Stout brownish bird with long, pouched beak, light-colored head and webbed feet.
Habitat: Coastal.
Comments: Slow flier that skims along the water's surface. Catches fish by plunging into the ocean. The white pelican (*Pelacanus erythrorhynchos*) – California's largest bird – is a common winter resident.

DOUBLE-CRESTED CORMORANT
Phalacrocorax auritus
Size: 30-36 in. (75-90 cm)
Description: Black bird distinguished by its slender neck, hooked bill and orange throat patch. Often perches with wings spread to allow them to dry. Head crests are rarely evident.
Habitat: Common in coastal waters, some found inland.
Comments: Nests in colonies on rocky ledges. Swims with bill pointed upward at an angle.

HERONS & ALLIES

Large wading birds with long legs, long necks and slender bills. Most inhabit marshes and other shallows where they feed on fish, frogs and insects. Sexes are similar. All fly with their necks folded into an 'S' curve.

Green Heron

Black-crowned Night-Heron

BLACK-CROWNED NIGHT-HERON
Nycticorax nycticorax
Size: 23-28 in. (58-70 cm)
Description: Distinguished by black crown and back, gray sides and tail and white underparts.
Habitat: Freshwater and brackish marshes.
Comments: Often seen at dusk and dawn stalking fish, amphibians and rodents in the shallow water. Another common California heron is the green heron (*Butorides virescens*).

GREAT BLUE HERON
Ardea herodias
Size: 40-52 in. (1-1.3 m)
Description: Large, slender bluish bird with long legs, a long, yellowish bill and white face. Black plumes extend back from the eye.
Habitat: Wetlands, margins of ponds, lakes and watercourses.
Comments: Often seen stalking fish and frogs in still waters.

GREAT EGRET
Ardea alba
Size: To 40 in. (1 m)

SNOWY EGRET
Egretta thula
Size: 20-27 in. (50-68 cm)
Description: Slender white wading birds. Great egret has a yellow bill and black feet. Snowy egret has a black bill and yellow feet.
Habitat: Marshes, lakes, estuaries.
Comments: The only other similar large white wading bird is the white morph of the great blue heron. It has yellow legs and a yellow bill.

Great Egret

Snowy Egret

GEESE

Geese are large, long-necked birds found near ponds and marshes. Highly terrestrial, they are often spotted grazing in fields and meadows. Their diet consists largely of grasses, grains and some aquatic plants. Noisy in flight, they are often heard before they're seen passing overhead.

CANADA GOOSE
Branta canadensis
Size: 24-45 in. (60-114 cm)
Description: Told by black head and neck, and white cheek patch.
Habitat: Near marshes, ponds, lakes and rivers.
Comments: Geese fly in a V-formation when migrating. Pairs usually mate for life. Call is a nasal – *honk.*

SNOW GOOSE
Chen caerulescens
Size: 25-31 in. (63-78 cm)
Description: White goose with an orange bill, orange feet and black wing tips.
Habitat: Marshes, sloughs, shallow lakes.
Comments: This arctic nester is a common winter resident. A dark phase of this species, called the blue goose, has a white head and a dark body.

DUCKS & ALLIES

Smaller than geese, ducks have shorter necks and are primarily aquatic. In most, breeding males are more brightly colored than females. Both sexes have a brightly-colored band (speculum) on the trailing edge of the wing.

MALLARD
Anas platyrhynchos
Size: 20-28 in. (50-70 cm)
Description: Male has green head, white collar and chestnut breast. Female is mottled brown. Both have a metallic blue speculum.
Habitat: Ponds and marshes.
Comments: The ancestor of domestic ducks. Call is a loud – *quack*.

NORTHERN PINTAIL
Anas acuta
Size: 20-30 in. (50-75 cm)
Description: Distinguished by its long neck and pointed tail. Male has a brown head and a white breast and neck stripe. Both sexes have a glossy brown speculum which is bordered in white.
Habitat: Shallow marshes and ponds.
Comments: Call is a short whistle.

GREEN-WINGED TEAL
Anas crecca
Size: 12-16 in. (30-40 cm)
Description: Male has chestnut head and a green eye patch. Female is brown-gray with a green speculum.
Habitat: Lakes and ponds.
Comments: Fast fliers that travel in tight flocks.

CINNAMON TEAL
Anas cyanoptera
Size: 14-17 in. (35-43 cm)
Description: Both sexes have a chalky blue forewing patch. Males are bright cinnamon; females are mottled brown.
Habitat: Marshes, shallow ponds and rivers.
Comments: The forewing patches are most visible in flight.

BLUE-WINGED TEAL
Anas discors
Size: 15-16 in. (38-40 cm)
Description: Male's white facial crescent is distinctive. Female has spotted sides. Note blue forewing in flight.
Habitat: Ponds, marshes, estuaries.
Comments: Small ducks winter in California.

AMERICAN WIGEON
Anas americana
Size: 18-23 in. (45-58 cm)
Description: Male is brownish with a gray head and a glossy green face patch. Female has a bluish bill and flecked head. Speculum is green.
Habitat: Freshwater streams, lakes, marshes.
Comments: Though primarily aquatic, these ducks can often be found nibbling grass on the shores of ponds and marshes.

NORTHERN SHOVELER
Anas clypeata
Size: 17-20 in. (43-50 cm)
Description: Told by its flat head and large, spatulate bill. Male has a green head, rusty sides and a blue wing patch.
Habitat: Fresh- and saltwater marshes, lakes, ponds.
Comments: Shovel-shaped bill is used to strain aquatic animals and vegetation from the water. Swims with bill pointed downward.

SURF SCOTER
Melanitta perspicillata
Size: 17-21 in. (43-53 cm)
Description: Black male has white patches on nape and forehead and a multi-colored bill. Female has two white cheek patches.
Habitat: Primarily coastal waters.
Comments: Often found in large flocks.

WOOD DUCK
Aix sponsa
Size: 17-21 in. (43-53 cm)
Description: Male is unmistakable. Note crested head of female.
Habitat: Woodland lakes, ponds, rivers.
Comments: One of the only ducks to nest in tree cavities.

RUDDY DUCK
Oxyura jamaicensis
Size: 15-16 in. (38-40 cm)
Description: Note broad bills and white cheeks. Tail is often cocked in the air when swimming.
Habitat: Lakes, ponds, rivers.
Comments: Common year-round.

COMMON MERGANSER
Mergus merganser
Size: 22-27 in. (55-68 cm)
Description: Told by sleek profile and long, slender bill. Male has an iridescent black-green head and white underparts. Female has a crested rufous head and a sharply defined white throat.
Habitat: Wooded lakes and rivers.
Comments: A diving duck, it feeds primarily on fish.

COOTS

Coots are chicken-billed birds often found in the company of ducks and geese. They are, however, more closely related to cranes than ducks.

AMERICAN COOT
Fulica americana
Size: 13-16 in. (33-40 cm)
Description: Dark bird with a chicken-like white bill, white rear, long greenish legs and lobed toes.
Habitat: Freshwater in the summer and fresh- and saltwater in winter.
Comments: Feeds on the shore and in the water. Habitually pumps its head back and forth when swimming.

HAWKS, EAGLES & ALLIES

Primarily carnivorous, these birds have sharp talons for grasping prey and sharply hooked bills for tearing into flesh. Many soar on wind currents when hunting. Sexes are similar in most.

CALIFORNIA CONDOR
Gymnogyps californianus
Size: 40-55 in. (1-1.38 m)
Description: Huge black bird with a naked head and hooked bill. White triangles on the underside of the wings are visible in flight.
Habitat: Mountains and open country.
Comments: An endangered species, it is the largest bird of prey in North America. Once nearly extinct, hand-raised populations have made a comeback in recent years and are slowly being transplanted in the wild.

TURKEY VULTURE
Cathartes aura
Size: 26-32 in. (65-80 cm)
Description: Large, brown-black bird with a naked red head. Trailing edge of wings are silvery.
Habitat: Dry, open country.
Comments: Feeds on carrion and is often seen along roadsides. Flys with wings held in a distinctive 'V' profile. Also called a buzzard.

GOLDEN EAGLE
Aquila chrysaetos
Size: 30-41 in. (75-104 cm)
Description: Large, dark soaring bird with long, broad wings. Its size distinguishes it from smaller hawks.
Habitat: Mountain regions.
Comments: Feeds on mammals, some birds and carrion. Often builds nests on power poles.

BALD EAGLE
Haliaeetus leucocephalus
Size: 30-43 in. (75-109 cm)
Description: Large dark bird with a white head and tail, and yellow legs and bill.
Habitat: Near water. Most common in northern California.
Comments: Feeds on fish and water birds. An endangered species, its local populations are well on the road to recovery.

OSPREY
Pandion haliaetus
Size: 20-24 in. (50-60 cm)
Description: Large hawk with dark brown back, light underparts and a dark eye stripe.
Habitat: Coastal waters, inland lakes and rivers.
Comments: Unlike most soaring birds, it glides with its wings arched. Often hovers over the water before diving after fish.

RED-TAILED HAWK
Buteo jamaicensis
Size: 20-25 in. (50-63 cm)
Description: Dark, broad-winged, wide-tailed hawk with light underparts and a red tail.
Habitat: Open fields and forests, farmlands.
Comments: This familiar hawk is often spotted perched on roadside telephone poles and fence posts.

NORTHERN HARRIER
Circus cyaneus
Size: 18-24 in. (45-60 cm)
Description: White rump is conspicuous in flight. Note V-shaped flight profile.
Habitat: Marshes, grasslands.
Comments: Flies a few feet above the ground, wavering from side to side as it hunts rodents and other small prey.

AMERICAN KESTREL
Falco sparverius
Size: 10-12 in. (25-30 cm)
Description: Small falcon with a rust back and tail, and pointed, narrow, spotted blue wings. Males have black facial marks.
Habitat: Wooded and open areas.
Comments: Formerly called the sparrow hawk. Often pumps tail when perching.

CHICKEN-LIKE BIRDS

Ground-dwelling birds that are chicken-like in looks and habit. Most have stout bills, rounded wings and heavy bodies. Primarily terrestrial, they are capable of short bursts of flight.

CALIFORNIA QUAIL
Callipepla californica
Size: 9-11 in. (23-28 cm)
Description: Plump bird with blue chest, black face and forward-curving plume (teardrop topknot).
Habitat: Mixed woodlands, open brushy areas, suburban parks.
Comments: Flocks descend on city parks and gardens after breeding season to feed on seeds and invertebrates.

California's State Bird

RING-NECKED PHEASANT
Phasianus colchicus
Size: 30-36 in. (75-90 cm)
Description: Told at a glance by its large size, long tail, green head and white neck ring. Female is mottled brown with a long tail.
Habitat: Brushy areas, farmland, woodland edges.
Comments: Widely introduced in the Central Valley.

PLOVERS

These wading birds are distinguished from sandpipers by their thick necks, short bills and large eyes. Active feeders, they characteristically move about in quick, short sprints. Sexes are similar.

KILLDEER
Charadrius vociferus
Size: 8-11 in. (20-28 cm)
Description: Brown bird with a white breast and two black neck bands. Rump shows orange in flight. Shrill call – *kill-dee* – is repeated continuously.
Habitat: Fields, pastures, parks, open areas.
Comments: Adults often feign injury to lure intruders away from their nesting area.

SHOREBIRDS

These birds are normally found along shores of oceans, lakes and ponds. Most have slender bills which they use to probe in sand and mud for invertebrates. This general grouping includes several distinct families of birds.

SANDERLING
Calidris alba
Size: 7-9 in. (18-23 cm)
Description: Plump, white-bellied shorebird with a black bill and legs. Upper plumage is rust in summer, gray in winter.
Habitat: Common on sandy shorelines and tidal flats.
Comments: Easily spotted on ocean shorelines running in and out with the waves. Feeds on tiny creatures that are beached as the waves recede.

SPOTTED SANDPIPER
Actitis macularia
Size: 6-8 in. (15-20 cm)
Description: Small brown bird with light, dark-spotted underparts and spindly, yellowish legs. Spots are evident during breeding season.
Habitat: Near water with vegetated shorelines.
Comments: A solitary bird, it teeters back and forth when walking. Flies with quivering wings held downward, alternating with low glides.

LEAST SANDPIPER
Calidris minutilla
Size: 5-7 in. (13-18 cm)
Description: A small brownish bird with a short, thin bill and yellowish legs.
Habitat: Mudflats, bogs, shorelines, wet fields.
Comments: A very common shorebird, it is relatively tame and can be closely approached. Call is – *peep.*

COMMON SNIPE
Gallinago gallinago
Size: 10-12 in. (25-30 cm)
Description: Stocky, long-billed shorebird with a spotted breast and streaked back.
Habitat: Marshes, ponds, bogs, wet fields.
Comments: When flushed it gives a sharp cry and flies off erratically.

LONG-BILLED CURLEW
Numenius americanus
Size: 20-26 in. (50-65 cm)
Description: Distinguished by its large size, buff-brown plumage and long, downcurved bill.
Habitat: Open areas near water.
Comments: Shows bright cinnamon wing linings in flight. Voice is a loud – *cur-lew!, cur-lew!*

MARBLED GODWIT
Limosa fedoa
Size: 16-20 in. (40-50 cm)
Description: Easily distinguished by its long upturned, black-tipped bill.
Habitat: Shorelines, mudflats.
Comments: Uses its long, sensitive bill to probe in sand and mud for worms and crustaceans.

WILLET
Catoptrophorus semipalmatus
Size: 14-17 in. (35-43 cm)
Description: Long-legged, long-billed gray shorebird. Wings flash black and white in flight.
Habitat: Shorelines, mudflats.
Comments: Noisy birds, their call sounds like – *pill-will-willet* or – *pee-wee-weee.*

AMERICAN AVOCET
Recurvirostra americana
Size: 15-20 in. (38-50 cm)
Description: Large shorebird with long legs and a long upcurved bill. Breeding birds have a tawny head and neck.
Habitat: Shallow ponds, marshes, mudflats.
Comments: Feeds by working bill side to side while walking through the water.

BLACK-NECKED STILT
Himantopus mexicanus
Size: 12-16 in. (30-40 cm)
Description: Very long-legged, black-and-white wader with a thin bill.
Habitat: Sea and lake shores, mudflats.
Comments: Common in fresh-and saltwater habitats.

BLACK OYSTERCATCHER
Haematopus bachmani
Size: 15-18 in. (38-45 cm)
Description: Black shorebird with a red bill.
Habitat: Rocky sea shores.
Comments: The stout bill is used to pry or break open shellfish. Call is a piercing whistle.

GULLS

These long-winged, web-footed birds are strong fliers and excellent swimmers. Adults are typically gray and white; immature birds are brownish. Most have square tails and are distinguished from each other by wing patterns and bill color.

CALIFORNIA GULL
Larus californicus
Size: 20-23 in. (50-58 cm)
Description: Told by its gray back, white-spotted, black wing tips and greenish legs.
Habitat: Inland lakes and ponds during breeding season, coastal shorelines in winter.
Comments: The similar ring-billed gull (*Larus delawarensis*), a common urban gull, has a dark ring on its bill.

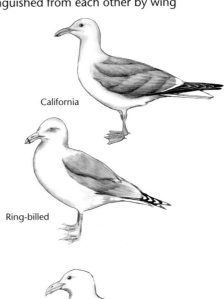

California

Ring-billed

WESTERN GULL
Larus occidentalis
Size: 24-27 in. (60-68 cm)
Description: Dark-backed gull with snowy-white underparts and pinkish legs.
Habitat: Coastal, rarely inland.
Comments: Varied diet includes carrion, garbage, eggs, young birds and aquatic animals.

DOVES

These familiar birds are common and widespread. All species coo. They feed largely on seeds, grain and insects.

ROCK PIGEON
Columba livia
Size: 12-13 in. (30-33 cm)
Description: Blue-gray bird with a white rump and black-banded tail. White, tan and brown variants also exist.
Habitat: Common in cities, towns and farmlands.
Comments: This introduced species is relatively tame and can be trained for homing.

MOURNING DOVE
Zenaida macroura
Size: 11-13 in. (28-33 cm)
Description: Slender, tawny bird with a long, pointed tail.
Habitat: Open woodlands, suburbs, farmlands.
Comments: Named for its mournful, cooing song. Feeds on the ground.

CUCKOOS & ALLIES

Members have long tails and curved bills. Sexes are similar.

GREATER ROADRUNNER
Geococcyx californianus
Size: 20-24 in. (50-60 cm)
Description: Long-legged, gray-brown bird with a crested head and long tail.
Habitat: Deserts, chaparral, open country.
Comments: A ground-dwelling bird that seldom flies. Feeds on small mammals, snakes and insects.

OWLS

These square-shaped birds of prey have large heads, large eyes and hooked bills. Large flattened areas around each eye help to amplify sound toward external ear flaps. Sexes are similar.

GREAT HORNED OWL
Bubo virginianus
Size: 20-25 in. (50-63 cm)
Description: Dark brown with heavily barred plumage, ear tufts, yellow eyes and white throat.
Habitat: Forests and woodlands.
Comments: Primarily nocturnal, it feeds on small mammals and birds. Sometimes spotted hunting during the day. Voice is a deep, resonant – hoo-hoo-hooooo.

GOATSUCKERS

These nocturnal insect-eaters have large, swallow-like heads. Ancients believed that the birds used their huge gaping mouths to suck the milk of goats.

COMMON NIGHTHAWK
Chordeiles minor
Size: 8-10 in. (20-25 cm)
Description: Told by large head, short bill, white wing bars and white throat. Long, pointed wings extend beyond the tail when perching.
Habitat: Forests, open country, cities.
Comments: Spectacular fliers, they can often be seen hawking for insects during daylight.

HUMMINGBIRDS

The smallest birds, hummingbirds are named for the noise made by their wings during flight. All have long needle-like bills and extensible tongues which are used to extract nectar from flowers.

ANNA'S HUMMINGBIRD
Calypte anna
Size: 3-4 in. (8-10 cm)
Description: Small, metallic-green bird. Male has red throat and forehead. Female has spotted throat.
Habitat: Chaparral, gardens, open woods.
Comments: When defending their territory, males will often swoop down to 'buzz' intruders. One of six species of hummingbirds found in California.

KINGFISHERS

Solitary, broad-billed birds renowned for their fishing expertise.

BELTED KINGFISHER
Ceryle alcyon
Size: 10-15 in. (25-38 cm)
Description: Stocky, crested blue-gray bird with a large head and bill.
Habitat: Near wooded ponds, lakes and rivers.
Comments: Often seen perched over clear water. Hovers over water before plunging in headfirst after fish.

WOODPECKERS

These strong-billed birds are usually spotted on tree trunks chipping away bark in search of insects. All have stiff tails which act like props as they forage. In spring, males drum on dead limbs and other resonant objects (e.g. garbage cans, drainpipes) to establish their territories. Seventeen species occur in California.

Downy

Hairy

DOWNY WOODPECKER
Picoides pubescens
Size: 5-7 in. (13-18 cm)
Description: A small, sparrow-sized, black-and-white woodpecker with a small bill. Males have a red head patch.
Habitat: Wooded areas.
Comments: Occurs in the same habitat as the similar, larger, hairy woodpecker (*Picoides villosus*).

ACORN WOODPECKER
Melanerpes formicivorus
Size: 8-10 in. (20-25 cm)
Description: A dark woodpecker with a yellowish face, red crown and a dark 'goatee'.
Habitat: Oak and pine forests.
Comments: Feeds on acorns and nuts. During fall harvest, it crams these fruits into tight holes to prevent theft by squirrels.

NORTHERN FLICKER
Colaptes auratus
Size: 10-14 in. (25-35 cm)
Description: Brownish woodpecker with a spotted breast and black bib. Note reddish wing linings; males have a red 'mustache'.
Habitat: Rural and urban woodlands, desert.
Comments: White rump patch is conspicuous in flight.

FLYCATCHERS

These compact birds characteristically sit on exposed perches and dart out to capture passing insects.

ASH-THROATED FLYCATCHER
Myiarchus cinerascens
Size: 7-9 in. (18-23 cm)
Description: Olive above, yellow below with a white throat and a rusty tail.
Habitat: Woodlands, deserts.
Comments: Often nests in cavities of rotting trees.

LARKS

Primarily terrestrial, slender-billed birds found in fields with low vegetation.

HORNED LARK
Eremophila alpestris
Size: 7-8 in. (18-20 cm)
Description: Brown bird with a yellow face, dark neck and eye marks and black 'horns.'
Habitat: Open areas including fields, shorelines, farmlands and parks.
Comments: Nests and feeds on the ground. Often found in flocks.

SWALLOWS

These acrobatic fliers have short bills, long pointed wings and long tails (often forked). Their wide mouths are adapted for scooping up insects on the wing. Seven species occur in California.

VIOLET-GREEN SWALLOW
Tachycineta thalassina
Size: 4-6 in. (10-15 cm)
Description: Plumage is glossy green-purple above, white below. White flank patches nearly meet above the tail.
Habitat: Open and semi-wooded areas in towns, farms and foothills.
Comments: Often seen perched in groups along power lines and fences. Flight is undulating and graceful.

CROWS & ALLIES

These large, omnivorous birds are very common. Sexes are similar.

STELLER'S JAY
Cyanocitta stelleri
Size: 12-14 in. (30-35 cm)
Description: Distinguished by its sooty plumage and prominent blue-gray head crest.
Habitat: Coniferous and pine-oak forests.
Comments: Very gregarious, it often frequents campsites and human dwellings in search of handouts.

WESTERN SCRUB-JAY
Aphelocoma californica
Size: 11-13 in. (28-33 cm)
Description: A streamlined blue bird with a long bill and tail. Key field marks are white throat, incomplete blue necklace and brown back.
Habitat: Oak-chaparral, woodlands.
Comments: Common in cities and towns. Flight is undulating and short, followed by a sweeping glide.

CLARK'S NUTCRACKER
Nucifraga columbiana
Size: 12-13 in. (30-33 cm)
Description: Light gray bird with a white face, long, sharply-pointed bill and long tail.
Habitat: Coniferous forests near the timberline.
Comments: Common near alpine campsites throughout the year, it occasionally wanders to low country in winter.

AMERICAN CROW
Corvus brachyrhynchos
Size: 18-21 in. (45-53 cm)
Description: Black bird with a thick black bill. Call is a distinct – *caw*.
Habitat: Fields, beaches, forests, parks, cities.
Comments: Abundant and widespread, they do a valuable service in controlling insect populations.

YELLOW-BILLED MAGPIE
Pica nuttalli
Size: 16-18 in. (40-45 cm)
Description: Large black-and-white bird with a long tail and a yellow bill.
Habitat: Woodlands, river valleys, farmlands, urban areas.
Comments: Found only in California, these gregarious birds are common at parks and picnic sites. The similar black-billed magpie (*Pica pica*) is common in eastern California.

COMMON RAVEN
Corvus corax
Size: 22-27 in. (55-68 cm)
Description: Similar to the crow, it is distinguished by its larger size, heavier beak, wedge-shaped tail and low, croaking call.
Habitat: Wilderness and open country.
Comments: An opportunistic feeder, it feeds on carrion and is often seen near garbage dumps.

NUTHATCHES

Nuthatches are stout little birds with thin, sharp bills and stumpy tails. They are usually spotted clambering about on tree trunks and branches.

WHITE-BREASTED NUTHATCH
Sitta carolinensis
Size: 5-6 in. (13-15 cm)
Description: Chunky, white-faced, grayish bird with black cap, white underparts and short, sharp bill.
Habitat: Coniferous and mixed wood forests.
Comments: Habitually creeps about on tree trunks and branches searching for insects, often descending head first. The red-breasted nuthatch (*Sitta canadensis*) is also common in California.

White-breasted

Red-breasted

WRENS

These little brown birds have the distinctive habit of cocking their tails in the air. They spend much of their time on the ground foraging for insects on leaves and branches. Eight species occur in California.

House

Marsh

HOUSE WREN
Troglodytes aedon
Size: 4-5 in. (10-13 cm)
Description: Distinguished by its barred tail, slender bill and cocked tail.
Habitat: Thickets, wooded areas, farmlands, towns.
Comments: An aggressive little bird, it moves about in quick, jerky motions, often scolding intruders. Common at birdbaths and feeders. The marsh wren (*Cistothorus palustris*) is common in cattail marshes and wetlands,

MOCKINGBIRDS & THRASHERS

Long-tailed birds with slender, downturned bills, they often sing loudly from exposed perches.

CALIFORNIA THRASHER
Toxostoma redivivum
Size: 10-13 in. (25-33 cm)
Description: Robin-sized gray-brown bird with long, downturned bill.
Habitat: Chaparral, parks, gardens.
Comments: Spends much of its time on the ground searching for insects and invertebrates.

NORTHERN MOCKINGBIRD
Mimus polyglottos
Size: 9-11 in. (23-28 cm)
Description: Robin-sized, gray-brown bird with a downturned bill and a long tail.
Habitat: Chaparral, scrubby woodlands, gardens.
Comments: Named for its habit of mimicking distinctive sounds like the calls of other birds.

CHICKADEES & TITMICE

These gregarious birds often flock together and are common at feeders.

CHESNUT-BACKED CHICKADEE
Poecile rufescens
Size: To 5 in. (13 cm)
Description: Distinguished by its black cap and bib and chestnut back and sides.
Habitat: Coniferous forests, lowlands.
Comments: Name-saying call is – *chick-a-dee-dee-dee.*

OAK TITMOUSE
Baeolophus inornatus
Size: To 5 in. (13 cm)
Description: Small grayish bird has a prominent head crest and pale under-parts.
Habitat: Oak woodlands, deciduous forests.
Comments: Call is a repeated two-note – *pe-ter* – or a chickadee-like – *chick-a-dee.*

THRUSHES

This group of woodland birds includes many good singers.

AMERICAN ROBIN
Turdus migratorius
Size: 9-11 in. (23-28 cm)
Description: Familiar to most, it is told by its gray back and rusty breast.
Habitat: Very common in towns, fields and open woodlands.
Comments: Forages on the ground for insects, snails and worms.

WESTERN BLUEBIRD
Sialia mexicana
Size: To 7 in. (18 cm)
Description: Male is bright blue above with a rusty breast and white belly. Female is brownish with dull blue wings and tail.
Habitat: Open woods, farmlands.
Comments: Often sits on conspicuous perches when hunting for insects. The sky-blue mountain bluebird (*Sialia currucoides*), is common in the Sierra Nevadas.

WAXWINGS

These gregarious birds are named for their red wing marks which look like waxy droplets.

CEDAR WAXWING
Bombycilla cedrorum
Size: 6-8 in. (15-20 cm)
Description: Told at a glance by its sleek, crested head, yellow belly, yellow-tipped tail and red wing marks.
Habitat: Open deciduous woods, orchards, suburbs.
Comments: Diet consists largely of berries and insects. Occurs in small flocks.

STARLINGS

These fat-bodied, short-tailed birds are abundant in cities and towns.

EUROPEAN STARLING
Sturnus vulgaris
Size: 6-9 in. (15-23 cm)
Description: Chubby bird with iridescent black-purple plumage and a pointed yellow bill.
Habitat: Farms, fields, cities, deserts.
Comments: Considered a pest by many, the starling is an aggressive bird that competes with native species for food and nesting sights. Usually travels in huge flocks.

WARBLERS & ALLIES

Members of this large family are distinguished from other small birds by their thin, pointed bills. Males tend to be more brightly-colored than females and are the only singers. Over 45 species occur in California.

YELLOW WARBLER
Dendroica petechia
Size: 4-5 in. (10-13 cm)
Description: Distinctive yellow bird with a streaked breast.
Habitat: Shrubs and thickets in river valleys, orchards and urban areas.
Comments: Song is a cheery – *sweet, sweet, sweet.*

YELLOW-RUMPED WARBLER
Dendroica coronata
Size: 5-6 in. (13-15 cm)
Description: Blue-gray bird with yellow rump and cap. Throat is white or yellow.
Habitat: Coniferous and mixed forests.
Comments: A relatively newly designated species, formerly the myrtle and Audubon's warblers.

'Myrtle' race

'Audubon's' race

ORANGE-CROWNED WARBLER
Vermivora celata
Size: 4-6 in. (10-15 cm)
Description: Drab olive bird with yellowish underparts and an orange crown patch.
Habitat: Open woodland, brushy areas.
Comments: Crown patch is often concealed.

COMMON YELLOWTHROAT
Geothlypis trichas
Size: 5-6 in. (13-15 cm)
Description: Male is olive green above, yellow below and has a white-bordered black mask.
Habitat: Moist grassy areas, marshes, thickets.
Comments: Song is a repeated – *wichity-wichy.*

BLACKBIRDS & ALLIES

A diverse group of birds ranging from iridescent black birds to brightly-colored meadowlarks and orioles. All have conical, sharply-pointed bills.

BROWN-HEADED COWBIRD
Molothrus ater
Size: 6-8 in. (15-20 cm)
Description: Blue-black bird with brown hood and finch-like bill.
Habitat: Open woods, farmlands and fields, often near domestic livestock.
Comments: Female is noted for her parasitic habit of laying eggs in the nests of other birds. While some species remove the new egg, most will raise the orphaned cowbird as their own, often at the expense of their own progeny.

Red-winged

Yellow-headed

RED-WINGED BLACKBIRD
Agelaius phoeniceus
Size: 7-10 in. (18-25 cm)

YELLOW-HEADED BLACKBIRD
Xanthocephalus xanthocephalus
Size: 8-11 in. (20-28 cm)
Description: Red-winged male is black with prominent red shoulder patches. Yellow-headed male is unmistakable.
Habitat: Sloughs, marshes and wet fields.
Comments: Usually nests in reeds or tall grass near water. Normally found in large flocks.

BULLOCK'S ORIOLE
Icterus bullockii
Size: 7-9 in. (18-23 cm)
Description: Distinctive black and orange bird has a black cap, chin and eyestripe and a white wing patch.
Habitat: Open deciduous forests, ranchlands.
Comments: Like most orioles, it weaves distinctive pouch-shaped nests out of grasses and twigs.

WESTERN MEADOWLARK
Sturnella neglecta
Size: 8-11 in. (20-28 cm)
Description: Mottled brown bird is distinguished by its bright yellow breast, white-edged tail, and dark V-shaped neckband.
Habitat: Grassy fields, meadows, marshes.
Comments: Loud, flute-like, gurgling song is distinctive.

TANAGERS

These brightly-colored birds of tropical orgin have heavy, conical, seed-cracking bills.

WESTERN TANAGER
Piranga ludoviciana
Size: 6-8 in. (15-20 cm)
Description: Yellow bird with a red head and dark back. Females and young are olive-colored with 2 light wing bars.
Habitat: Open coniferous and mixed forests.
Comments: Gregarious bird is common near picnic areas. Call is a dry – *pit-ick, pit-ick.*

FINCHES, SPARROWS & ALLIES

Members of this family are brightly-colored and have short, thick, seed-cracking bills.

AMERICAN GOLDFINCH
Carduelis tristis
Size: 4-6 in. (10-15 cm)
Description: Male is bright yellow with a black cap, black tail and wings and a white rump. Duller female lacks a cap.
Habitat: Wooded groves, gardens.
Comments: Often found in flocks. Can be identified on the wing by its deeply undulating flight. Canary-like song is bright and cheery.

HOUSE FINCH
Carpodacus mexicanus
Size: 5-6 in. (13-15 cm)
Description: Brown bird with a reddish forehead, breast and rump.
Habitat: Cities, towns, open country, bottomlands.
Comments: Highly social birds, they are easily attracted to feeders and nesting sites.

PINE SISKIN
Carduelis pinus
Size: 4-5 in. (10-13 cm)
Description: Brown bird with heavily streaked plumage and a notched tail. Small yellow patches on wings and tail are most prominent in flight.
Habitat: Coniferous and mixed forests.
Comments: Quite tame and easily attracted to feeders. Often found flocking in the tops of trees.

LAZULI BUNTING
Passerina amoena
Size: 5-6 in. (13-15 cm)
Description: Distinguished by turquoise head and back, cinnamon breast and white belly.
Habitat: Deciduous forests, chaparral.
Comments: Song is a series of repeated notes such as – *sweet-sweet, chew-chew.*

SONG SPARROW
Melospiza melodia
Size: 5-7 in. (13-18 cm)
Description: Distinguished by heavily-streaked breast with streaks converging to a central spot. Tail is rounded.
Habitat: Very common in bushes and woodlands near water.
Comments: Often visits feeders and birdbaths. Forages along the ground. Melodious song usually begins with 3-4 similar notes.

CHIPPING SPARROW
Spizella passerina
Size: 5-6 in. (13-15 cm)
Description: Told by red cap, white eyebrow line, unstreaked breast and notched tail.
Habitat: Open forests, fields, lawns, gardens.
Comments: Nests are often victimized by brown-headed cowbirds which lay their eggs there for the sparrows to raise. Song is a repetitive, sharp – *chip.*

SPOTTED TOWHEE
Pipilo maculatus
Size: To 8 in. (20 cm)
Description: Told by black hood, rufous sides, white belly and red eyes. Female is brown where male is black.
Habitat: Woodlands, wood margins, cities, usually in undergrowth.
Comments: Its dull-brown cousin, the brown towhee (*Pipilo fuscus*), is also common in woods and gardens.

DARK-EYED JUNCO
Junco hyemalis
Size: 5-7 in. (13-18 cm)
Description: Key field marks are dark head, whitish bill, white belly and white-edged tail. Has gray sides and a gray back or a black head and a brown back.
Habitat: Coniferous and mixed woods, gardens, parks.
Comments: Gregarious and easily attracted to feeders. A relatively newly designated species, formerly the slate-colored junco, Oregon junco, gray-headed Junco and white-winged junco. Of these, only the first 2 occur in California.

'Slate-colored' race

'Oregon' race

WEAVER FINCHES

These sparrow-like birds were introduced to North America in 1850, and are now widespread throughout the continent.

HOUSE SPARROW
Passer domesticus
Size: 5-6 in. (13-15 cm)
Description: Black throat and brown nape of male are key field marks. Females and young are dull brown with a light eye stripe.
Habitat: Suburbs, cities, farmlands.
Comments: These gregarious, social birds gather in large flocks between breeding seasons.

WHAT ARE REPTILES & AMPHIBIANS?

Reptiles and amphibians represent a diverse array of water- and land-dwelling animals.

REPTILES

Reptiles can generally be described as terrestrial, scaly creatures that breathe through lungs. The majority reproduce by laying eggs on land; in some, the eggs develop inside the mother who later gives birth to live young. Contrary to popular belief, very few are harmful to man; all are valuable in controlling rodent and insect populations.

The most common types of California reptiles are turtles, lizards and snakes.

AMPHIBIANS

Amphibians are smooth-skinned, limbed vertebrates that live in moist habitats and breathe through lungs, skin, gills, or a combination of all three. While they spend much of their lives on land, they still depend on a watery environment to complete their life cycle. Most reproduce by laying eggs in or near water. The young hatch as swimming larvae – tadpoles, for example – which breathe through gills. After a short developmental period, the larvae metamorphose into young adults with lungs and legs.

The most common types of California amphibians are salamanders, frogs and toads.

HOW TO IDENTIFY REPTILES AND AMPHIBIANS

Reptiles are secretive but can be observed if you know where to look. Turtles are found on the edges of ponds and lakes and often sun themselves on rocks and logs. Lizards sun themselves in habitats ranging from open deserts to suburban back yards and are easily the most conspicuous reptiles. The best time to look for snakes is in the early morning or late afternoon when it's not too hot. Look in meadows, fields, woods, or on the margins of ponds, checking under sun-warmed logs and rocks where they may be resting.

Of the amphibians, frogs and toads are probably the easiest to observe since they loudly announce their presence during breeding season. Frogs are found in wet areas on or near the water. Toads are more terrestrial and may be found far from water, especially during the day. Salamanders are more secretive and rarely venture out of their cool, moist habitats.

Caution – When seeking reptiles, watch where you step. Many snakes are well-camouflaged and can be sluggish in the morning or after eating. Also, be careful where you put your hands. Do not put hands in places you can't see into. Turn over rocks and logs with a stick or tool.

TURTLES

Turtles are easily distinguished by their large bony carapaces (shells), which serve to protect them from most predators. Like all reptiles, turtles breathe air through lungs; they are also able to breathe underwater from gill-like respiratory surfaces on the mouth and anus. Turtles are most active in spring during mating season. Most are omnivores and eat a wide variety of plant and animal matter.

DESERT TORTOISE
Gopherus agassizii
Size: 10-15 in. (25-38 cm)
Description: Distinguished by its brown, dome-shaped shell and thick, stumpy legs.
Habitat: Dry, sandy areas in southeast California.
Comments: A protected species. It typically feeds at dawn and dusk and lies in a shallow burrow throughout the day.

California's State Reptile

WESTERN POND TURTLE
Clemmys marmorata
Size: 4-7 in. (10-18 cm)
Description: Told by its dark, streamlined shells. Inconspicuous lines or flecks radiate from the center of each shell segment.
Habitat: Ponds, quiet streams, marshes, ditches.
Comments: Often basks in the sun on partially submerged rocks or logs. Feeds on vegetation, crutaceans and insects.

RED-EARED SLIDER
Chrysemys scripta
Size: 5-11 in. (13-28 cm)
Description: Distinguished by its round, yellow-marked shell and wide, red ear stripes.
Habitat: Ponds, quiet streams, marshes, ditches.
Comments: The common pet store turtle. Many have been introduced to the wild by their owners and may out-number native turtles in some areas.

LIZARDS

Lizards are scaly-skinned animals which usually have four legs and a tail, movable eyelids, visible ear openings, claws and toothed jaws. A few species are legless and superficially resemble snakes. They represent the largest group of living reptiles and range in size from tiny skinks to the giant 10 foot-long monitor lizards of Indonesia. Over 3,000 species are found worldwide, 95 of which occur in the U.S.

Most lizards lay eggs on or in the ground. The incubation period depends largely on the ambient temperature and the hatchlings are independent from birth. In a few species, the female retains the eggs until the young are ready to hatch.

CALIFORNIA WHIPTAIL
Cnemidophorus tigris mundus
Size: 8-12 in. (20-30 cm)
Description: Slim, light-striped lizard with long, slender tail. Dark blotches on sides and throat.
Habitat: Chaparral, deserts and open forests throughout much of northern California.
Comments: Diurnal and often encountered. Moves in jerky steps, with head darting side to side.

WESTERN SKINK
Eumeces skiltonianus
Size: 7-9 in. (18-23 cm)
Description: Cylindrical, lizard-like creature has broad dorsal stripe edged in black. Juveniles have a blue tail.
Habitat: Woodlands and forests under ground litter.
Comments: Most active in the late afternoon. Like many lizards, its tail readily detaches when grasped by a predator; in such instances the detached tail wiggles, providing a diversion which often allows the tail-less skink to escape. The tail grows back in a few weeks.

WESTERN BANDED GECKO
Coleonyx variegatus
Size: 5-6 in. (13-15 cm)
Description: Banded lizard with protruding eyes.
Habitat: Rocky and sandy areas.
Comments: The most vocal of lizards, its call is a cricket-like – *chirp.*

SIDE-BLOTCHED LIZARD
Uta stansburiana
Size: 4-7 in. (10-18 cm)
Description: Small brownish lizard with
a blotched back and sides. Several variants exist, all of which have a prominent dark spot behind each front leg.
Habitat: Arid and semi-arid regions
with rocky or sandy soil and low-
growing plants.
Comments: Primarily ground-dwelling,
it feeds on insects during the day.

WESTERN FENCE LIZARD
Sceloporus occidentalis
Size: 6-9 in. (15-23 cm)
Description: Spiny-scaled, brown-green
or black lizard with blue patches on
neck, sides and belly.
Habitat: Rocky areas, mixed forests,
near buildings and fences.
Comments: Active during the day,
it is often encountered. Will display blue
undersides to attract females or defend
territory.

SOUTHERN ALLIGATOR LIZARD
Gerrhonotus multicarinatus
Size: 10-17 in. (25-43 cm)
Description: Green to gray lizard
with an elongate, stiff body, long tail
and distinctive skin fold down each
side.
Habitat: Found under ground litter
in cool, moist woodlands.
Comments: Active during the day,
it feeds largely on insects and snails.
A good swimmer.

COLLARED LIZARD
Crotaphytus collaris
Size: 9-14 in. (23-35 cm)
Description: Greenish, long-tailed
lizard with two dark collar markings.
Habitat: Rocky areas in deserts,
foothills and forests.
Comments: It flees danger by run-
ning swiftly on its hind legs. Will bite
readily if handled.

SNAKES

Snakes are limbless reptiles with moist, scaly skin, toothed jaws, no ear openings or eyelids and a single row of belly scales. They move by contracting their muscles in waves and undulating over the ground. All are carnivorous and swallow their prey whole. They flick their tongues in and out constantly to 'taste' and 'smell' the air around them. Most continue to grow in length during their life and shed their outer skin periodically. The vast majority are harmless to humans.

WESTERN YELLOWBELLY RACER
Coluber constrictor mormon
Size: 2-6 ft. (60-180 cm)
Description: Slender, smooth scaled snake is brown to bluish above and yellowish to whitish below.
Habitat: Favors open areas including meadows, roadsides, prairies, forest glades, chaparral.
Comments: Active during the day, racers are fast-moving and good climbers. Often seen crossing roads. Holds its head and neck high when foraging.

COMMON KINGSNAKE
Lampropeltis getulus californiae
Size: 3-7 ft. (1-2.1 m)
Description: Large brown-black snake with light crossbands; light dorsal stripe may also be visible.
Habitat: Forests, rocky slopes, swamps, prairie, meadows, farmlands.
Comments: Active in mornings and afternoons, it hunts at night during hot weather. Diet consists of small mammals, rodents, lizards and snakes (including rattlers!).

MONTEREY RINGNECK SNAKE
Diadophis punctatus vandenburghi
Size: 10-30 in. (25-75 cm)
Description: Small, slender snake has a red neck ring. Belly scales are also red.
Habitat: Moist areas, grasslands.
Comments: Common snake has secretive habits and hides under rocks and in crevices.

WESTERN AQUATIC GARTER SNAKE
Thamnophis couchi
Size: 20-57 in. (50-143 cm)
Description: Six subspecies of this highly-variable snake are found in California. Most have a weak dorsal stripe and blotched sides. Others have distinct back and side stripes. All are aquatic and primarily diurnal.
Habitat: Rivers, streams and marshes throughout California.
Comments: Feeds on fish, amphibians and invertebrates.

CALIFORNIA RED-SIDED GARTER SNAKE
Thamnophis sirtalis infernalis
Size: 20-52 in. (50-130 cm)
Description: Dark snake with red blotches between its light dorsal and side stripes.
Habitat: Near water in meadows, farmlands and valleys.
Comments: Commonly encountered during the day. One of several subspecies of common garter snake, most of which have red blotches on their sides.

PACIFIC GOPHER SNAKE
Pituophis melanoleucus catenifer
Size: 3-8 ft. (.9-2.5 m)
Description: Large, yellow-cream snake with dark blotches on its back and sides.
Habitat: Found in a variety of habitats (excluding swamps) from mountains to lowlands.
Comments: Though non-poisonous, it imitates a rattlesnake when threatened by coiling up, hissing loudly, vibrating its tail, and striking out at its aggressor. Eats primarily small rodents and is valued for pest control on farms.

WESTERN RATTLESNAKE
Crotalus viridis
Size: 1-5 ft. (30-150 cm)
Description: A darkly-blotched, greenish-brown snake with a spade-shaped head, defined neck and tail rattle.
Habitat: Grasslands, brushy areas and woodlands from sea level to 11,000 ft. (3,350 m).
Comments: A pit viper, it has heat sensing areas between its eyes and nostrils which help it detect prey. Enlarged front fangs have hollow canals which inject poison into prey when it strikes. Eats mostly rodents.

SALAMANDERS

Salamanders are smooth-skinned, tailed creatures that lack claws and ear openings. Some have the ability to regenerate tails or limbs lost to predators. Seldom seen, they live in dark, moist habitats and are nocturnal and secretive. They are most active in the spring and fall, especially near the pools where they breed.

Fertilization in most is internal but is not accomplished by copulation. During mating, the male releases a small packet of sperm which the female brushes against and draws into her body. The packet is kept in her body until she ovulates, which may be months later. Most species lay their eggs in water. Both adults and larvae are carnivorous and feed on worms and insects and other invertebrates.

CALIFORNIA NEWT
Taricha torosa
Size: 5-8 in. (13-20 cm)
Description: Warty skin is red-brown above, yellow to orange below. Breeding males have smooth skin.
Habitat: Near water in oak and pine woodlands.
Comments: When disturbed it assumes a defensive posture, exposing its brightly-colored undersides. Most likely to be seen on cool, wet days.

CALIFORNIA SLENDER SALAMANDER
Batrachoseps attenuatus
Size: 3-6 in. (8-15 cm)
Description: Blackish, worm-like salamander has a yellow, red or brown dorsal stripe, tiny limbs and dark, white-speckled belly.
Habitat: Under moist leaf litter and logs in grasslands and woodlands.
Comments: The most common salamander in California. Easiest to spot during rainy weather.

CALIFORNIA TIGER SALAMANDER
Ambystoma californiense
Size: 6-9 in. (15-23 cm)
Description: Black salamander is covered with cream or yellowish spots.
Habitat: Open woodlands and grasslands near water.
Comments: Most visible during breeding season from January to February.

NORTHWESTERN SALAMANDER
Ambystoma gracile
Size: 6-9 in. (15-23 cm)
Description: Gray-brown salamander with a ridged tail and prominent swellings behind its eyes.
Habitat: Moist forests and grasslands.
Comments: A mole salamander, it spends much of its time underground feeding on worms, insects and small animals.

PACIFIC GIANT SALAMANDER
Dicamptodon ensatus
Size: 7-12 in. (18-30 cm)
Description: Large, smooth-skinned salamander has marbled brown-to-purplish coloration.
Habitat: Near waterways, in cool forests in northern California.
Comments: Lives under logs, rocks and forest litter.

FROGS & TOADS

Frogs and toads are squat amphibians common near ponds and lakes. All have large heads, large eyes, long hind legs and long, sticky tongues that they use to catch insects. Most have well-developed ears and strong voices. Only males are vocal.

Frogs have smooth skin, slim waists and many have prominent dorsal ridges. In most, the male initiates mating by calling for females. When he finds a mate, he clasps her in water and fertilizes the eggs as they are laid. The eggs initially hatch into fish-like tadpoles that breathe through gills and feed on vegetation. They later transform into young adults with limbs and lungs.

Toads can be distinguished from frogs by their dry, warty skin and prominent glands behind their eyes (parotoids). Some also have swellings between their eyes (bosses). When handled roughly by would-be predators, the warts and glands secrete a toxic substance that makes the toads extremely unpalatable. Contrary to popular belief, handling toads does not cause warts.

PACIFIC TREEFROG
Hyla regilla
Size: 1-2 in. (2-5 cm)
Description: A dark green-to-tan frog, it is distinguished by its black eye stripe and large toe pads.
Habitat: Near water under shelter of grass or brush, from sea level to 10,000 ft. (3,000 m).
Comments: Largely nocturnal, it is the most commonly heard frog. Call is familiar to the movies, a high-pitched, two-part – *kreck-ek*, the last syllable rising.

RED-LEGGED FROG
Rana aurora
Size: 2-5 in. (5-13 cm)
Description: Red-brown to gray frog has a light jaw stripe. Belly and inside of legs are reddish. Has well-developed folds of skin down its back.
Habitat: Damp, densely vegetated areas and woodlands.
Comments: Primarily diurnal. Call is a stuttering series of guttural growls lasting 2-3 seconds.

BULLFROG
Rana catesbeiana
Size: 4-8 in. (10-20 cm)
Description: Large green-brown frog with large ear openings.
Habitat: Ponds and lakes with ample vegetation.
Comments: Nocturnal, it is often seen along shorelines. Voice is a deep-pitched – *jug-o-rum*. An introduced species.

NORTHERN LEOPARD FROG
Rana pipiens
Size: To 5 in. (13 cm)
Description: Brown to green frog has light-edged dark spots. Snout is relatively pointed. A ridge of skin runs from behind the eye to the groin.
Habitat: Marshes, waterways, wet meadows.
Comments: Call is a rattling snore. Primarily nocturnal.

WESTERN SPADEFOOT TOAD
Scaphiopus hammondi
Size: 1-3 in. (3-8 cm)
Description: Brown-gray-green toad covered with random dark blotches. Skin is covered in small bumps that are tipped in red or orange. Glossy, black wedge-shaped spade on each hind foot is used to excavate burrows.
Habitat: Grassy plains, gravelly flats.
Comments: Lives in deep burrows and is primarily nocturnal. Rolling call resembles a cat's purr.

CALIFORNIA TOAD
Bufo boreas halophilus
Size: 2-5 in. (5-13 cm)
Description: Gray-green toad with light dorsal stripe and warts framed by black blotches.
Habitat: Meadows, woodlands and valleys near water.
Comments: Call sounds like peeping chick. Nocturnal, it is active during the day in cooler weather.

WHAT ARE FISHES?

Fishes are cold-blooded vertebrates that live in water and breathe dissolved oxygen through organs called gills. They are generally characterized by their size, shape, feeding habits, and water temperature preference. Most live in either saltwater or freshwater, though a few species divide their lives between the two (these are referred to as anadromous fishes).

All fishes have streamlined bodies covered in scales, and swim by flexing their bodies from side to side. Their fins help to steer while swimming and can also act as brakes. Many species possess an internal air bladder which acts as a depth regulator. By secreting gases into the bladder or absorbing gases from it, they are able to control the depth at which they swim.

Most fish reproduce by laying eggs freely in the water. In many, the male discharges sperm over the eggs as they are laid by the female. Depending on the species, eggs may float, sink, become attached to vegetation, or be buried.

HOW TO IDENTIFY FISHES

First, note the size, shape and color of the fish. Are there any distinguishing field marks like the double dorsal fins of the basses or the downturned lips of the suckers? Is the body thin or torpedo-shaped? Note the orientation and placement of fins on the body. Consult the text to confirm identification.

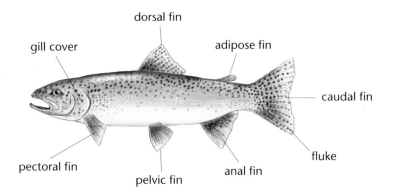

LAMPREYS

Lampreys are members of the most primitive order of fishes. All lack jaws and feed on the blood and tissue of other fishes.

PACIFIC LAMPREY
Lampetra tridentata
Size: To 30 in. (75 cm)
Description: Identified by its slender eel-like body, round gill openings and sucker-like mouth.
Habitat: Lampreys hatch in freshwater and spend their adult life in marine habitats.

Comments: Feeds by attaching itself by the mouth to a host fish, rasping a hole in its side with its horny teeth and sucking out nourishment.

SHARKS & ALLIES

These fishes lack bones and have skeletons completely composed of cartilage. They also lack an internal air bladder and must swim continuously or sink to the bottom.

SPINY DOGFISH
Squalus acanthias
Size: To 5 ft. (1.5 m)
Description: Gray-brown shark that lacks an anal fin and has a spine at the front of each dorsal fin. Sides often covered with light spots.
Habitat: Shallow water to depths of 120 ft. (36 m).

Comments: Very common in coastal waters and considered a pest by anglers.

LEOPARD SHARK
Triakis semifasciata
Size: To 7 ft. (2.1 m)
Description: Gray-brown shark with prominent dark spots.
Habitat: Common in shallow bays with sandy or rocky bottoms.

Comments: Often found in large schools, it is a popular food fish that is harvested commercially.

BAT RAY
Myliobatis californica
Size: To 6 ft. (1.8 m)
Description: Brown-green flat fish with a large, elevated head, long wings and a long, whip-like tail.
Habitat: Shallow waters with sandy bottoms.
Comments: Venomous stinger near base of tail can inflict a painful injury. A popular sport fish.

STURGEONS

Members of this prehistoric group are among the largest freshwater fishes in North America, reaching sizes to 20 ft. (6 m) and 3,200 lbs. (1,450 kg). Some live for up to 150 years.

WHITE STURGEON
Acipenser transmontanus
Size: To 13 ft. (3.9 m)
Description: Size and shape are key field marks. Note mouth barbels (whiskers).
Habitat: Feeds along the bottom in deep water.
Comments: These large fishes are found primarily in brackish water, though some move to the ocean. All spawn in freshwater.

HERRINGS & ALLIES

Found in large schools, they are important forage and bait fishes.

PACIFIC HERRING
Clupea pallasii
Size: To 18 in. (45 cm)
Description: Greenish above, silvery below, with a short dorsal fin and a deeply-forked tail.
Habitat: Inshore waters.
Comments: Quantities of sticky eggs (roe) are deposited on kelp and intertidal vegetation during spawning. Huge quantities of eggs are harvested for Asian markets.

NORTHERN ANCHOVY
Engraulis mordax
Size: To 9 in. (23 cm)
Description: Blue-green above, silvery below, with a snout projecting beyond the mouth.
Habitat: Nearshore waters, usually in dense schools.
Comments: Common bait fish that is harvested commercially for its meat and oil.

SALMON & TROUT

This diverse group includes many popular sport fishes. Most have robust bodies, square caudal fins, an adipose fin and strong teeth. Trout are found primarily in fresh water; salmon are anadromous and live in saltwater for one or more years before returning to freshwater to spawn.

COHO (SILVER) SALMON
Oncorhynchus kisutch
Size: To 39 in. (98 cm)
Description: Back and upper lobe of caudal fin are black-spotted. Breeding male is green-blue above and white below with brick red sides. At sea, color is silvery.
Habitat: Anadromous.
Comments: They spend 2-3 years at sea before returning to spawn.

Oceanic phase

Breeding

CHINOOK (KING) SALMON
Oncorhynchus tshawytscha
Size: To 5 ft. (1.5 m)
Description: Blue-to-green above, it has irregular black spots on its back and caudal fin. Gums are black at base of teeth.
Habitat: Anadromous.
Comments: The largest salmon, it can weigh over 100 lbs. (45 kg). Spawns in spring and fall and enters freshwater throughout the year.

Oceanic phase

Breeding

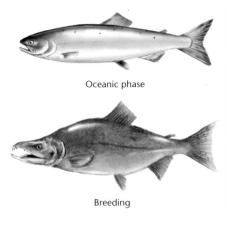

Oceanic phase

Breeding

SOCKEYE (RED) SALMON
Oncorhynchus nerka
Size: To 33 in. (83 cm)
Description: Blue-green above, and silvery below, it lacks dark spots on its back or fins. Spawning male has bright red body, green head, humped back and hooked jaw.
Habitat: Anadromous.
Comments: Formerly widespread, its spawning grounds are now limited to waters north of the Sacramento River. Populations of sockeye that become landlocked in freshwater are called kokanee.

Oceanic phase

Breeding

CHUM (DOG) SALMON
Oncorhynchus keta
Size: To 40 in. (1 m)
Description: This salmon lacks black spots and has a slender caudal peduncle. Distinguished from the sockeye by its white-edged lower fins. Spawning male has blotchy red sides.
Habitat: Anadromous.
Comments: Also called dog salmon, it spawns in streams close to the ocean in late fall and winter.

BROOK TROUT
Salvelinus fontinalis
Size: To 28 in. (70 cm)
Description: Colorful greenish fish with blue-haloed, red side spots and wavy light lines on back and dorsal fin. Lower fins are reddish.
Habitat: Clear, freshwater streams and rivers; some are anadromous.
Comments: An introduced sport fish weighing up to 14 lbs. (6.3 kg).

RAINBOW TROUT
Oncorhynchus mykiss
Size: To 45 in. (1.14 m)
Description: A silvery, dark-spotted fish named for the distinctive reddish band running down its side. Band is most prominent during spring spawning.
Habitat: Abundant in streams, reservoirs and lakes.
Comments: A very important game fish. The sea-run version of this species is called steelhead.

Rainbow

Steelhead

BROWN TROUT
Salmo trutta
Size: To 40 in. (1 m)
Description: Brown fish covered with black and red spots.
Habitat: Cool streams and lakes; some are anadromous.
Comments: An introduced species renowned for its wariness.

GOLDEN TROUT
Oncorhynchus aguabonita
Size: To 28 in. (70 cm)
Description: Brilliantly-colored trout is dark above, yellow below, with bright red markings on its sides, belly and cheeks. Dorsal and caudal fins are covered with large, black spots.
Habitat: Primarily mountain lakes and streams.
Comments: Originally found in only the Kern River, it has been widely introduced throughout the state at high elevations.

California's State Fish

MINNOWS & ALLIES

These fishes can be distinguished from similar species by their lack of an adipose fin and toothless jaws. Lips are typically thin and tail is well-forked.

GOLDFISH
Carassius auratus
Size: To 16 in. (40 cm)
Description: Thick gray-brown fish with large scales and a long dorsal fin.
Habitat: Sluggish streams, muddy ponds, sloughs.
Comments: Native to China, they are tolerant of warm and polluted waters. Domesticated goldfish are the more familiar orange color.

COMMON CARP
Cyprinus carpio
Size: To 30 in. (75 cm)
Description: A large-scaled, deep-bodied olive fish, it is identified by its long dorsal fin, mouth barbels (whiskers) and forked, orangish tail. Dorsal fin has a single spine.
Habitat: Found in clear and turbid streams, ponds and sloughs. Prefers warm water.
Comments: Widely distributed throughout the U.S.; introduced to California.

CALIFORNIA ROACH
Hesperoleucus symmetricus
Size: To 4 in. (10 cm)
Description: Gray-blue above and light below with speckled sides and a dark side stripe. Lips and fin bases are red-orange in mature fish.
Habitat: Creeks, small rivers and tributaries.
Comments: Very common in coastal streams.

SPECKLED DACE
Rhinichthys osculus
Size: To 4 in. (10 cm)
Description: Highly variable, it is usually a dusky, gray-olive fish with a black-speckled body and distinct side stripe.
Habitat: Pools, streams, rivers.
Comments: There are numerous subspecies of this widespread, common minnow.

GOLDEN SHINER
Notemigonus crysoleucas
Size: To 12 in. (30 cm)
Description: Deep-bodied, narrow fish with a silver-olive sides and light-colored fins. Often has a dark side stripe.
Habitat: Vegetated pools, streams, rivers and ponds.
Comments: Common bait fish often found in schools near the shore. A non-native species introduced throughout California.

SUCKERS

Suckers have distinctive, downturned fleshy lips that they use to 'vacuum' the bottom of lakes and streams in search of invertebrates.

SACRAMENTO SUCKER
Catostomus occidentalis
Size: To 24 in. (60 cm)
Description: Brown-green above, yellowish below with downturned lips. Breeding male has a reddish side stripe.
Habitat: Clear pools, streams, lakes.
Comments: Unlike many bottom-feeding fishes, suckers lack mouth barbels (whiskers).

CODFISHES

All have long tapered bodies and long dorsal and anal fins. Barbels are often present.

PACIFIC HAKE
Merluccius productus
Size: To 3 ft. (90 cm)
Description: Elongate, silvery fish with jutting lower jaw and sharp teeth. Second dorsal and anal fins are notched.
Habitat: Open sea from surface to depths of 3,000 ft. (914 m).
Comments: Often caught by anglers trolling for salmon.

LIVEBEARERS

Livebearers are fertilized internally and give birth to live young.

MOSQUITOFISH
Gambusia affinis
Size: To 2.5 in. (6 cm)
Description: Olive-brown above, yellowish below with 1-3 rows of dark spots on dorsal fin and tail.
Habitat: Fresh- and saltwater ponds, lakes, slow-moving streams.
Comments: Feeds on mosquito larvae and has been widely introduced throughout California.

STICKLEBACKS

These small fishes are named for the defined row of spines along their back. Noted for their mating behavior, the males are responsible for building intricate, suspended nests and guarding the eggs and young.

THREESPINE STICKLEBACK
Gasterosteus aculeatus
Size: To 4 in. (10 cm)
Description: Slender green fish distinguished by the row of 3 short spines ahead of the dorsal fin.
Habitat: Found in shallow, vegetated streams, pools and small lakes.
Comments: Diet consists of crustaceans, insects and algae.

None

TEMPERATE BASSES

Found in fresh- and saltwater, they are important commercial and sport fishes.

STRIPED BASS
Morone saxatilis
Size: To 6 ft. (1.8 m)
Description: Olive to blue-gray fish with 6-9 dark side stripes.
Habitat: Nearshore waters.
Comments: Introduced to the west coast in the late 1800s, it is now widespread and common.

SUNFISHES

Members all have two joined dorsal fins separated by a notch. Popular sport fishes, they have been widely introduced throughout California.

LARGEMOUTH BASS
Micropterus salmoides
Size: To 38 in. (95 cm)
Description: Greenish, mottled fish with a dark, often blotched, side stripe. Has a large mouth with the upper jaw extending past the eye.
Habitat: Quiet, vegetated lakes, ponds and rivers.
Comments: A very popular sport fish that is taken with live and artificial bait. The similar smallmouth bass (*M. dolomieu*) has blotched sides and its jaw does not extend beyond the eye.

Largemouth

Smallmouth

BLUEGILL
Lepomis macrochirus
Size: To 16 in. (40 cm)
Description: Flattened, brassy fish with long pectoral fins and a dark-spotted dorsal fin. Side bars are usually visible. Body color ranges from blue to yellow.
Habitat: Quiet, vegetated lakes, ponds and rivers.
Comments: One of the most popular panfishes in the country.

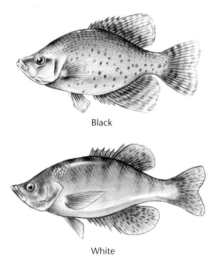

Black

White

BLACK CRAPPIE
Pomoxis nigromaculatus
Size: To 16 in. (40 cm)
Description: Gray-green, mottled fish with a hunched back. Dorsal fin is set well back and has 7-8 spines on its leading edge.
Habitat: Quiet, clear lakes, ponds and rivers.
Comments: Another non-native species that has been widely introduced in Arizona, the white crappie (*P. annularis*), also common in California, has 6 spines in its first dorsal fin.

TUNA & ALLIES

A diverse family of mostly streamlined, fast-moving fishes with torpedo-shaped bodies, pointed snouts and deeply forked tails. Many are important commercially.

PACIFIC MACKEREL
Scomber japonicus
Size: To 25 in. (63 cm)
Description: Dark blue to green above, silvery below with numerous black bars down its back.
Habitat: Nearshore waters to 50 miles offshore.
Comments: Swims in large schools and is common in nearshore waters. An important commercial food fish.

PACIFIC BONITO
Sarda chiliensis
Size: To 3 ft. (90 cm)
Description: Green-blue above, silvery below with 5-11 dark, oblique stripes on body.
Habitat: Nearshore waters to 30 miles offshore.
Comments: Swims in schools near the surface. Feeds on herring and other schooling fishes.

ALBACORE
Thunnus alalunga
Size: To 5 ft. (1.5 m)
Description: Dark blue to gray above, grayish below. Note long pectoral fin.
Habitat: Offshore waters.
Comments: Popular sport fish is abundant off the California coast in summer.

YELLOWTAIL
Seriola lalandi
Size: To 5 ft. (1.5 m)
Description: A large, silvery fish with a yellowish side stripe and yellow, forked tail.
Habitat: Offshore waters.
Comments: One of California's most popular sport fishes, up to 400,000 are taken by anglers annually.

WRASSES

Family of colorful, buck-toothed tropical fishes.

CALIFORNIA SHEEPHEAD
Semicossyphus pulcher
Size: To 3 ft. (90 cm)
Description: Told by black head and rear, red middle and white chin.
Habitat: Shallow waters in southern California.
Comments: Common along rocky shores.

BARRACUDAS

Slender, silvery fishes with two widely-spaced dorsal fins and long snouts.

CALIFORNIA BARRACUDA
Sphyraena argentea
Size: To 4 ft. (1.2 m)
Description: Slender blue-gray or brown fish with a long snout, jutting lower jaw and prominent teeth.
Habitat: Offshore waters to depths of 60 ft. (18 m).
Comments: Up to one million of these prized sport fish are harvested annually.

DAMSELFISHES

Family of nearshore fishes that are often brightly-colored.

GARIBALDI
Hypsypops rubicundus
Size: To 14 in. (35 cm)
Description: Bright orange fish with a deeply-notched tail.
Habitat: Nearshore waters from Monterey Bay south.
Comments: It is illegal to spear or retain this protected species in California.

SURFPERCHES

Flattened fishes with a long dorsal fin. Several species are frequently caught by surf anglers along the coast.

STRIPED SEAPERCH
Embiotoca lateralis
Size: To 12 in. (30 cm)
Description: A colorful fish told by its blue and orange side stripes.
Habitat: Offshore waters.
Comments: Over 100,000 are taken annually by anglers and spearfishers.

ROCKFISHES

Most members of this large family have prominent, spiky dorsal fins and large eyes. Spines of the dorsal, anal and pelvic fins are venomous and can cause painful injury.

VERMILION ROCKFISH
Sebastes miniatus
Size: To 30 in. (75 cm)
Description: Reddish above, light red or orange below with red fins. Older individuals have gray marks on their head and back.
Habitat: Shallow to deep rocky reefs.
Comments: An excellent food fish popular in restaurants.

BLACK-AND-YELLOW ROCKFISH
Sebastes chrysomelas
Size: To 15 in. (38 cm)
Description: Black-and-yellow blotched rockfish.
Habitat: Nearshore water to depths of 120 ft. (36.5 m).
Comments: Valued food fish often found near kelp beds.

LINGCOD

Fishes with long bodies and long dorsal and anal fins.

LINGCOD
Ophiodon elongatus
Size: To 5 ft. (1.5 m)
Description: Large green-brown fish with a jutting lower jaw and a long, spiny, notched dorsal fin.
Habitat: Nearshore waters.
Comments: A very important commercial and sport fish.

FLATFISHES

Flattened fishes with both eyes on the same side of the body. They often lie on the sea bottom buried in sediment with only their eyes exposed.

STARRY FLOUNDER
Platichthys stellatus
Size: To 3 ft. (90 cm)
Description: Right- or left-eyed. Dorsal and anal fin have dark and orangish bars.
Habitat: Mostly nearshore waters.
Comments: Related to numerous similar species of flatfishes found off the California coast, including dover sole (*Microstomus pacificus*).

CALIFORNIA HALIBUT
Paralichthys californicus
Size: To 5 ft. (1.5 m)
Description: Right-eyed flat fish with long dorsal and anal fins.
Habitat: Offshore waters.
Comments: An important commercial and sport fish in northern waters.

WHAT IS SEASHORE LIFE?

This section includes a variety of animal and plant groups that can be found along the west coast of California. Most species can be readily observed in tidal pools or shallow waters. All of the animals in this section are classed as invertebrates or animals without backbones.

The best time to observe the greatest variety of species is during low tide. Tide times are often published in newspapers, and tide tables are available at most sporting goods stores. There are generally two tides a day, and tidal differences may be as much as 15 ft. (4.5 m). The lowest tides of the year occur in midwinter and midsummer.

The groups covered in this section include marine plants, coelenterates, sea stars and allies, crustaceans and mollusks.

High Tide   9-15 ft. (2.7-4.5 m)

rockweed
barnacles
limpets
shore crabs

Mid Tide   5-8 ft. (1.5-2.4 m)

sea urchins
sea stars
clams
oysters
snails
sand dollars

Low Tide   3-4 ft. (0.9-1.2 m)

kelp
eelgrass
crabs
sea stars
anemones
sea urchins
sand dollars
scallops

Subtidal Zone   0-3 ft. (0-.9 m)

SEASHORE PLANTS

This general group includes a few of the most common coastal marine plants.

BULL KELP
Nereocystis luetkeana
Size: To 65 ft. (20 m)
Description: Long, tubular stem is anchored to the bottom and supported by a round float. Long, bladed, brownish leaves radiate from the float along the water's surface.
Habitat: Found in dense beds along shorelines to depths of 100 ft. (30 m).
Comments: Kelp beds provide an important source of food and cover for invertebrates, fishes and mammals.

ROCKWEED
Fucus distichus
Size: To 20 in. (50 cm)
Description: A ragged, brownish plant with swollen air bladders along a ribbed stem.
Habitat: Rocky shorelines.
Comments: Very widely distributed.

EELGRASS
Zostera marina
Size: To 5 ft. (1.5 m)
Description: Tall slender plant with grass-like leaves.
Habitat: Muddy and sandy soils.
Comments: Leaves are often encrusted with animals and insects. Surfgrass (*Phylospadix*) is more common than eelgrass south of Santa Barbara.

SEA PALM
Postelsia palmaeformis
Size: To 2 ft. (60 cm)
Description: Resembles a palm tree with drooping leaves.
Habitat: Intertidal.
Comments: Sea palm, eelgrass and surfgrass all have special protection under the Fish and Game Code.

COELENTERATES

This group contains a variety of free-swimming and colonial creatures including jellyfish, hydroids, anemones and corals.

GIANT GREEN ANEMONE
Anthopleura xanthogrammica
Size: To 10 in. (25 cm)
Description: Flattened green disk with numerous, uniform tentacles.
Habitat: Very common in tide pools on exposed shores.
Comments: Algae living in the tissues of the anemone are responsible for its color.

BROODING ANEMONE
Epiactis prolifera
Size: To 2 in. (5 cm)
Description: Identified by its flower-like profile. Color ranges from red-pink to green.
Habitat: Commonly found at low tide attached to eelgrass and rocks.
Comments: Terminal mouth is surrounded by up to 90 stinging tentacles which are withdrawn when it is disturbed.

MOON JELLYFISH
Aurelia aurita
Size: To 16 in. (40 cm)
Description: Told by white, translucent, bell-shaped body with fringe of numerous, stinging tentacles.
Habitat: Found floating on the surface of the water or washed ashore.
Comments: Stings can cause an itchy rash. Like all jellyfish, it swims by expelling water from its mouth.

SAIL JELLYFISH
Velella velella
Size: To 3 in. wide (8 cm)
Description: Small jellyfish has a translucent triangular crest on its upper surface that acts like a sail.
Habitat: Surface of the ocean.
Comments: Also called by-the-wind-sailor, it can 'tack' like a sailboat.

SEA STARS & ALLIES

These mostly bottom-dwelling animals are characterized by spiny bodies and radial symmetry, i.e., body parts repeat around a central hub, as in a wheel. The 'arms' are usually arranged in multiples of 5, and may be short or long, cylindrical or flattened. Size indicates width.

OCHRE SEA STAR
Pisaster ochraceus
Size: To 10 in. (25 cm)
Description: Identified by its short rays and patterned surface. Body color may be purple, yellow, orange or brown.
Habitat: Common in tidepools and attached to rocks at low tide.
Comments: Like most sea stars, it is capable of regenerating severed body parts.

GIANT SPINED SEA STAR
Pisaster giganteus
Size: To 12 in. (30 cm)
Description: Large sea star may be red, brown tan or purple. Delicate spines have blue rings around their base.
Habitat: Found on rocks during low tides.
Comments: Although sea stars have no jaws, most are carnivorous and very destructive to shellfish populations.

PURPLE SEA URCHIN
Strongylocentrotus purpuratus
Size: To 4 in. (10 cm)
Description: Told by its red-purple color, rounded body and long spines.
Habitat: Rocky shores below the low tide line.
Comments: It is commercially harvested for its gonads which are considered a sushi delicacy. Urchin skeletons are frequently washed ashore.

Skeleton

SAND DOLLAR
Dendraster excentricus
Size: To 3 in. (8 cm)
Description: Hard brown body is covered with short spines. Note flower-like impression on shell.
Habitat: Found at low tides on sandy beaches, often partially buried.
Comments: Skeletons of dead sand dollars are often found washed ashore.

Skeleton

CRUSTACEANS

Like insects, crustaceans have a hard external skeleton, antennae and paired limbs. The limbs differ greatly in form and function, and are modified for specific purposes in different species. Most live in water.

PURPLE SHORE CRAB
Hemigrapsus nudus
Size: To 2 in. (5 cm)
Description: Distinguished by its deep purple body and red-spotted claws. Red-brown, green and yellow variants also exist.
Habitat: Beneath rocks in protected waters.
Comments: Often found scuttling about on intertidal rocks.

ACORN BARNACLE
Balanus spp.
Size: To 1 in. (3 cm)
Description: A small white-gray, heavily-ribbed shell that often grows in clusters attached to rocks and piers at the high tide line.
Habitat: Very common throughout coastal California.
Comments: Barnacles hatch as free-swimming larvae which eventually attach themselves to solid objects and mature into shelled adults. They feed by opening plates at the top of their shells and extending feathery arms to trap small organisms.

RED CRAB
Cancer productus
Size: To 6 in. (15 cm)
Description: Distinguished by fan-shaped shell and brick-red color.
Habitat: Rocky shores, estuaries.
Comments: Young crabs are highly variable in color and often have streaked shells.

DUNGENESS CRAB
Cancer magister
Size: To 9 in. (23 cm)
Description: Large red-brown crab.
Habitat: Young are found in sandy pools near low-tide line; older individuals gradually migrate into deeper waters.
Comments: This is the crab often found in markets. Locally abundant.

HERMIT CRAB
Pagurus **spp.**
Size: To 1 in. (3 cm)
Description: Small crab lives in discarded snail shell. Has two pair of walking legs.
Habitat: Common intertidally in tide pools or on mud or sand.
Comments: The crab sheds replaces its shell as it grows larger.

MOLLUSKS

This large group of soft-bodied and usually hard-shelled invertebrates occupies many habitats in water and on land. The mouth of most mollusks – excluding bivalves – has a ribbon-like toothed structure called a radula which helps the animals break down food or capture prey.

ROUGH KEYHOLE LIMPET
Diodora aspera
Size: To 2 in. wide (5 cm)
Description: Cone-shaped shell has side ribs and a hole in the top.
Habitat: Found intertidally on kelp and rocks.
Comments: Color of shell ranges from white to tan and gray and is influenced by the kinds of animals that colonize the shell surface.

BLACK TURBAN SNAIL
Tegula funebralis
Size: To 1.5 in. (4 cm)
Description: Thick, purplish-black shell
houses a black snail.
Habitat: Abundant at low tides on
exposed shores.
Comments: Limpets often attach them-
selves to its shell to feed on the algae
that collect there.

CALIFORNIA HORN SNAIL
Cerithidea californica
Size: To 1.5 in. (4 cm)
Description: Stout, spire-like shell has
10-11 whorls. Color is usually brown,
although some are almost black.
Habitat: Mud flats.
Comments: Very common on mud flats
when the tide is out.

BLACK ABALONE
Haliotis cracherodii
Size: To 6 in. (15 cm)
Description: Large, oval shell is black,
blue or green. Interior is pearly white.
Note row of holes on outside of shell.
Habitat: High-tide mark to 20 ft.
(6 m) depth.
Comments: Although abundant, it has
little commercial value. Its larger cousin,
the red abalone (*Haliotis rufescens*), is
the species typically served in local
restaurants.

NATIVE LITTLENECK CLAM
Protothaca staminea
Size: To 3 in. (8 cm)
Description: Rounded, white shell
is ribbed with growth lines.
Habitat: Sandy and gravelly soils
in the mid-tide region.
Comments: Feeds by extracting
minute particles from the water
passing over its gills.

GIANT PACIFIC OYSTER
Crassostrea gigas
Size: To 12 in. (30 cm)
Description: Distinguished by its heavy, irregular shell.
Habitat: Common in the intertidal zone.
Comments: Like other bivalves (including clams, mussels and scallops), its body is composed of two hinged shells held together by powerful muscles. Most live in sand or mud.

CALIFORNIA MUSSEL
Mytilus californianus
Size: To 10 in. (25 cm)
Description: Thick, oval-shaped, blue-black shell has prominent ridges.
Habitat: Intertidal waters, rock crevices.
Comments: Very abundant along rocky coasts.

BLUE MUSSEL
Mytilus edulis
Size: To 4 in. long (10 cm)
Description: Blue-black shell is oval-shaped and relatively smooth.
Habitat: Intertidal waters.
Comments: Common on exposed shores. Often found attached to pilings and other marine objects.

PACIFIC PINK SCALLOP
Chlamys hastata
Size: To 3 in. (8 cm)
Description: Beautiful fan-shaped shell is often covered with colored sponges and may be white, yellow, orange, purple or pink.
Habitat: Intertidal waters.
Comments: Unlike other bivalves, scallops possess a set of eyes that line the edge of the shell.

WHAT ARE TREES & SHRUBS?

TREES

Trees can be broadly defined as perennial woody plants at least 16 ft. (5 m) tall with a single stem and a well-developed crown of branches, twigs and leaves. Most are long-lived plants and range in age from 40-50 years for smaller deciduous trees to several hundred years for many of the conifers.

A tree's size and shape is largely determined by its genetic makeup, but growth is also affected by environmental factors such as moisture, light and competition from other species. Trees growing in crowded stands will often only support compact crowns due to the competition for light. Some species at high altitudes grow gnarled and twisted as a result of exposure to high winds.

Common Tree Silhouettes

| Pine | Juniper | Willow | Oak | Cottonwood |

SHRUBS

Shrubs are perennial woody plants normally less than 16 ft. (5 m) tall that support a crown of branches, twigs and leaves. Unlike trees, they are anchored to the ground by several stems rather than a single trunk. Most are fast-growing and provide an important source of food and shelter for wildlife.

N.B. – *Some shrubs that are most conspicuous when in bloom are included in the following section on flowering plants.*

HOW TO IDENTIFY TREES AND SHRUBS

First, note its size and shape. Does it have one or several 'trunks.' Examine the size, color, and shape of the leaves and how they are arranged on the twigs. Are they opposite or alternate? Simple or compound? Hairy or smooth? Are flowers or fruits visible on branches or on the ground? Once you've collected as much information as you can, consult the illustrations and text to confirm your sighting.

SIMPLE LEAF SHAPES

| Elliptical | Heart-shaped | Rounded | Oval | Lobed | Lance-shaped |

COMPOUND LEAVES

Leaflets

LEAF ARRANGEMENTS

| Alternate | Opposite | Whorled |

COMMON FRUITS

Drupe
junipers, cherries,
dogwoods, hollies

Pome
apples, plums,
yuccas, pears

Nut
walnuts, pecans,
hickories

Berry-like
blackberries,
oranges, tomatoes

Winged Seed
dandelions,
milkweeds,
poplars,
cottonwoods

Samara
maples, ashes,
hophornbeams,
elms

Acorn
oaks

Pod
peas, mesquites,
locusts

YEWS

Yews are a primitive race of needle-leaved evergreen trees that lack woody cones.

CALIFORNIA TORREYA
Torreya californica
Size: 20-70 ft. (6-21 m)
Description: Stiff, evergreen leaves are flattened with a sharp tip and grow in 2 rows along twigs. Plum-like fruit contains a large brown seed.
Habitat: Mixed evergreen forests and exposed slopes in northern California.
Comments: This highly aromatic tree is also called the stinking cedar owing to the offensive odor released by crushed leaves.

PACIFIC YEW
Taxus brevifolia
Size: To 50 ft. (15 m)
Description: Shrub or tree has a rounded crown. Soft, flat needles grow in 2 rows along twigs. Red berries have protruding greenish seeds.
Habitat: Shady coniferous and mixed forests.
Comments: Most parts of the plant is poisonous.

PINES

Most have long, needle-like leaves which grow grouped in bundles of two to five. Male and female cones usually occur on the same tree.

LODGEPOLE PINE
Pinus contorta
Size: 65-80 ft. (20-24 m)
Description: Crown is ragged and slender, straight trunk is often barren when shaded. Stiff needles are twisted into bundles of 2 and cone scales have a single prickle near their outer edge.
Habitat: Bogs, alpine forests, sandy soils.
Comments: Named for its straight trunk which Native Americans used for teepee poles. Cones are stimulated to open by heat and this is often one of the first trees to reseed burned-out areas following forest fires.

WESTERN WHITE PINE
Pinus monticola
Size: 50-100 ft. (15-30 m)
Description: Straight trunk supports a ragged, conical crown of horizontally growing branches. Blue-green needles are arranged in clusters of 5. Long-stalked, elongate cones are up to 15 in. (38 cm) long.
Habitat: Found in mixed and pure stands in the northern Sierra Nevada mountains.
Comments: One of the largest pines, its wood is highly desirable since it is of a uniformly high grade.

BRISTLECONE PINE
Pinus aristata
Size: 20-40 ft. (6-12 m)
Description: Needles are arranged into tight bundles of 5 that grow curved around the twig. Purplish cones bristle with stiff, recurved prickles.
Habitat: Dry, rocky exposed slopes in eastern California.
Comments: The oldest living trees on earth, with some specimens over 4,500 years old. Found in the Inyo National Forest.

PONDEROSA PINE
Pinus ponderosa
Size: 50-130 ft. (15-40 m)
Description: Stout, stiff needles are up to 8 in. (20 cm) long and grouped in bundles of 2 or 3. Oval cones have scales that terminate in sharp prickles.
Habitat: Widespread in mountain regions, usually in pure stands.
Comments: Very common and an important timber tree. Most common at elevations between 3,000-5,000 ft. (900-1,500 m).

SUGAR PINE
Pinus lambertiana
Size: 100-160 ft. (30-49 m)
Description: Sharply pointed blue-green needles are bundled in 5's. Elongate stalks are 12-24 in. (30-60 cm) long.
Habitat: Mixed coniferous forests.
Comments: The largest American pine, it is named for its sweet sap. Trunks may be up to 10 ft. (3 m) in diameter.

SINGLELEAF PINYON PINE
Pinus monophylla
Size: 15-30 ft. (4.5-9 m)
Description: Small, often shrubby pine with spreading, rounded branches. Stiff needles grow singly along twigs. Short-stalked, rounded cones produce large seeds that are sold as pine nuts.
Habitat: Dry, gravelly and rocky soils.
Comments: One of four species of pinyon pines found in the southwestern states.

FIRS

Firs are medium-sized evergreens with dense crowns. Flattened, stalkless needles grow singly and bear a longitudinal scar from base to tip. Cones grow upright from branches and disintegrate when seeds are ripe. After the cone scales are shed, a central, candle-like stalk remains on the branch.

WHITE FIR
Abies concolor
Size: 100-160 ft. (30-49 m)
Description: Flexible needles are flat and blunt-tipped, and grow to the sides or curve upward. Cylindrical cones are green, purple or yellow and up to 5 in. (13 cm) long.
Habitat: Moist soils in pure or mixed stands with other firs.
Comments: An important food source for deer, grouse, porcupines, rodents and birds. Firs often have symmetrical crowns and are prized Christmas ornamentals.

DOUGLAS-FIRS

Larger than true firs, Douglas-firs are easily identified by their shaggy cones.

DOUGLAS-FIR
Pseudotsuga menziesii
Size: 100-250 ft. (30-76 m)
Description: Flexible needles grow along twigs that terminate in red buds. Cones are distinguished at a glance by the 3-pointed bracts protruding between scales. Side branches in the crown droop.
Habitat: Moist, well-drained soils from sea level to 9,000 ft. (2,750 m).
Comments: One of the tallest and most important timber trees in the U.S.

REDWOODS & ALLIES

The large size of these famous trees is attributed to their resistance to disease, fire and insects. Both the redwood and sequoia are found primarily in California.

REDWOOD
Sequoia sempervirens
Size: 200-300 ft. (61-92 m)
Description: A very tall tree with a straight trunk, red-brown fibrous bark and an open, irregular crown. Trunk diameter is typically 10-15 ft. (3-5 m). Tiny cones are 1 in. (3 cm) long.
Habitat: Moist soils and bottomlands in the coastal fog belt.
Comments: The world's tallest tree is also California's state tree. Once widespread, surviving members are now protected in a number of national and state parks.

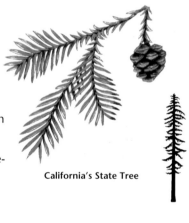

California's State Tree

GIANT SEQUOIA
Sequoiadendron giganteum
Size: 150-250 ft. (46-76 m)
Description: Huge thick-trunked tree with fibrous red bark. Scale-like leaves are tightly bunched along twigs. Trunk is deeply furrowed at base.
Habitat: Rocky soils at elevations above 4,500 ft. (1,370 m) in central California.
Comments: Considered the largest trees on earth (in mass), exceptional specimens are over 270 ft. (82 m) tall and 3,800 years old.

CEDARS & ALLIES

All have scaly or awl-shaped leaves which are tightly bunched together on twigs. The heavily-weighted twigs usually droop at their tips and give the plants a relaxed profile. Most cedar wood is very fragrant.

INCENSE-CEDAR
Libocedrus decurrens
Size: 50-150 ft. (15-46 m)
Description: Large tree with fibrous, brown bark. Long, scale-like leaves are arranged in small, vase-shaped whorls along twigs, lumpy to the touch. Oblong cones are composed of 6 flattened scales that open when ripe.
Habitat: Mountain slopes between 1,000-8,000 ft. (300-2,400 m).
Comments: An aromatic tree, it is an important source of timber for siding, shakes, chests and pencils.

WESTERN RED CEDAR
Thuja plicata
Size: To 175 ft. (53 m)
Description: Large tree has drooping branches covered with overlapping scale-like leaves. Red-brown bark is fibrous and shredding. Small cones have woody scales.
Habitat: Coniferous forests in extreme northwestern California.
Comments: Bark is resistant to rot and is often used for shingles and siding.

MONTEREY CYPRESS
Cupressus macrocarpa
Size: 50-80 ft. (15-24 m)
Description: Picturesque coastal tree has a flat-topped, irregular crown and twisted trunk in exposed areas. Scale-like leaves have blunt tips.
Habitat: Exposed coastal headlands.
Comments: Young trees growing in protected areas have symmetrical crowns. Native to the Monterey Bay region, it has been widely introduced throughout California.

CALIFORNIA JUNIPER
Juniperus californica
Size: To 40 ft. (12 m)
Description: Shrub or small tree with a branching, irregular crown. Scale-like needles grow in 3's along twigs. Bluish, berry-like fruits are often conspicuous.
Habitat: Dry slopes throughout the mountains and foothills, semi-desert areas.
Comments: In desert regions, it is often associated with pinyon pines and Joshua trees.

WILLOWS & ALLIES

Most have narrow, finely-toothed leaves which grow alternately along twigs. Flowers often appear in spring, before the leaves, along semi-erect catkins. After pollination, flowers are succeeded by small pods. When ripe, these pods burst open and shed numerous cottony seeds in the wind.

ARROYO WILLOW
Salix lasiolepis
Size: To 30 ft. (9 m)
Description: Shrub or small tree with an irregular crown of erect branches. Lance-shaped, long leaves are finely-toothed.
Habitat: Wet soils along arroyos (gulches, gullies) and streams.
Comments: Noted for their extensive root systems, willows are often instrumental in preventing soil erosion along stream banks.

WEEPING WILLOW
Salix babylonica
Size: To 40 ft. (12 m)
Description: Easily distinguished by its short trunk and wide crown of drooping (weeping) branches. Narrow, finely-toothed leaves are evident from early spring until late autumn.
Habitat: Moist soils, along streams.
Comments: Native to China, this introduced willow is widely planted as an ornamental throughout California.

POPLARS

Found in moist habitats, these fast-growing trees are distinguished from willows by their drooping flower clusters (catkins). Alternate, unlobed leaves are toothed, generally heart-shaped and usually as long as they are broad. Green-white bark of young trees becomes grayish and furrowed as it matures.

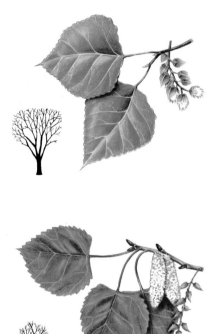

FREMONT COTTONWOOD
Populus fremontii
Size: 50-80 ft. (15-24 m)
Description: Has a large, broad crown of spreading branches. Heart-shaped leaves have gently-toothed edges and flattened stems. Reddish flowers bloom in drooping catkins and are succeeded by capsules containing cottony seeds.
Habitat: Wet soils near water.
Comments: In dry areas, cottonwoods indicate the presence of underground water.

TREMBLING ASPEN
Populus tremuloides
Size: To 70 ft. (21 m)
Description: Long, slender trunk supports a crown of spreading branches. Rounded leaves have long stems and the leaves rustle (tremble) in the slightest breeze. Leaves turn yellow in autumn.
Habitat: Well-drained soils in a variety of habitats.
Comments: Its twigs, leaves, catkins and bark are an important food source for wildlife.

LOMBARDY POPLAR
Populus nigra
Size: 30-60 ft. (9-18 m)
Description: Distinguished by its narrow crown of short, erect branches. Leaves are roughly triangular.
Habitat: Moist soils.
Comments: Introduced from Europe, it is now widely planted throughout California as an ornamental.

BIRCHES

Leaves are commonly oval-shaped with toothed margins. Distinctive, cylindrical, woody cones (strobiles) disintegrate in the fall when ripe. All are fast-growing and short-lived.

EUROPEAN WHITE BIRCH
Betula pendula
Size: To 50 ft. (15 m)
Description: Distinguished by its crown of drooping branches. Leaves are rounded-triangular with toothed margins. Bark is papery and peels off in strips.
Habitat: Moist soils.
Comments: Grows rapidly and is planted throughout California.

ALDERS

Alders are fast-growing shrubs and trees with ragged crowns and deeply veined leaves. Their fruit is a distinctive woody cone.

WHITE ALDER
Alnus rhombifolia
Size: To 70 ft. (21 m)
Description: Tree with a rounded crown of spreading branches. Alternate leaves are saw-toothed and up to 4 in. (10 cm) long.
Habitat: Near streams to 8,000 ft. (2,400 m) elevation.
Comments: Easily distinguished in winter when yellow male catkins dangle from leafless twigs.

MAPLES

Maples are distinguished by their fan-shaped leaves and winged seed pairs.

BIGLEAF MAPLE
Acer macrophyllum
Size: To 70 ft. (21 m)
Description: Large leaves, to 8 in. (20 cm) have 3 lobes. Drooping flower clusters are succeeded by V-shaped winged seed pairs.
Habitat: Woodlands, canyons.
Comments: Fast-growing species is often found near waterways. Leaves turn yellow in autumn.

OAKS

Oaks represent a group of important hardwoods. Generally, they are large trees with stout trunks and spreading crowns that produce acorns for fruit.

CALIFORNIA WHITE OAK
Quercus lobata
Size: 60-100 ft. (18-30 m)
Description: Large tree with a stout trunk and widely spreading branches. Leaves have 7-11 rounded lobes and are up to 4 in. (10 cm) long. Acorns are slim and conical.
Habitat: Rich soils in valleys and foothills.
Comments: Common throughout California's interior and central coast range, its acorns are a valuable source of food for birds and mammals.

CALIFORNIA BLACK OAK
Quercus kelloggii
Size: 40-80 ft. (12-24 m)
Description: Large tree with a round crown. Leaves have 5 to 7 deeply-toothed lobes and are up to 6 in. (15 cm) long. Rounded acorns have a scaly cup.
Habitat: Dry, well-drained soils in foothills and mountains.
Comments: Its leaves distinguish it from other oaks. A popular source of firewood.

CALIFORNIA LIVE OAK
Quercus agrifolia
Size: 30-80 ft. (9-24 m)
Description: Evergreen with a spreading crown of branches and a stout trunk. Leaves are oblong and arched upward. Acorns are conical.
Habitat: Slopes and valleys.
Comments: The common oak along the coast.

CALIFORNIA SCRUB OAK
Quercus dumosa
Size: To 25 ft. (7.6 m)
Description: Shrub or small tree with small, oval, evergreen leaves. Acorns have a thick, scaly cup.
Habitat: Dry, barren areas.
Comments: A major component of the chaparral community, it often grows in thickets.

LAURELS

Mostly aromatic trees and shrubs providing camphor, cinnamon, and aromatic oils.

CALIFORNIA LAUREL
Umbellularia californica
Size: 40-80 ft. (12-24 m)
Description: Tree with short trunk supporting large rounded crown. Narrow leathery leaves exude a spicy scent when crushed. Clusters of yellow spring flowers are succeeded by greenish-purple berries that ripen in autumn.
Habitat: Moist, fertile soils from sea level to 6,000 ft. (1,800 m).
Comments: Commonly planted as an ornamental tree along the coast.

SYCAMORES

Large trees with very stout trunks and distinctive 'buttonball' fruits.

CALIFORNIA SYCAMORE
Platanus racemosa
Size: 40-80 ft. (12-24 m)
Description: Massive trunk supports a broad crown of spreading branches. The bark flakes off in irregular patches so it appears white-brown at first glance. Leaves have 5 lobes and are somewhat star-shaped. Fruit consists of a ball of numerous seeds supported on stiff upright hairs.
Habitat: Moist soils along streams in valleys and canyons.
Comments: One of three sycamores native to the U.S.

ROSES & ALLIES

A variable family of trees and shrubs found throughout North America.

BITTER CHERRY
Prunus emarginata
Size: To 20 ft. (6 m)
Description: Leaves are oval or lance-shaped and taper to a point. White flowers bloom in spring in round, flat-topped clusters and are succeeded by small, bright red berries.
Habitat: Found in dry to moist soil in coastal region and the Sierra Nevadas.
Comments: The fruit is extremely bitter and not edible.

MOUNTAIN MAHOGANY
Cercocarpus betuloides
Size: To 20 ft. (6 m)
Description: Shrub or small tree with a spreading crown. Toothed, evergreen leaves are elliptical with a narrow base. Yellowish flowers are succeeded by fruits with a feathery plume at the tip.
Habitat: Dry mountain slopes, chaparral.
Comments: The term *cercocarpus* is derived from the Greek words for 'tail' and 'fruit.'

TOYON
Heteromeles arbutifolia
Size: To 30 ft. (9 m)
Description: A beautiful tree or shrub with a short trunk and a spreading, round crown. Thick, oblong, evergreen leaves are sharply-toothed. White flowers bloom in dense clusters in early summer and are succeeded in autumn by small, red apple-like fruits.
Habitat: Slopes, canyons and streamsides to 4,000 ft. (1,200 m).
Comments: Fruits persist into winter and are very showy.

CHAMISE
Adenostoma fasciculatum
Size: 3-7 ft. (.9-2.1 m)
Description: Wiry shrub or small tree with dark brown, shredding bark and bundled, needle-like leaves. Clusters of tiny white flowers bloom at stem tips in spring.
Habitat: Chaparral, foothills.
Comments: Also called greasewood for its oily, stringy wood.

PEAS & ALLIES

Most members of this large family of trees, shrubs and herbs produce fruit in seed pods.

HONEY MESQUITE
Prosopis glandulosa
Size: To 20 ft. (6 m)
Description: Shrub or small tree with crown of crooked branches. Leaves are up to 10 in. (25 cm) long and have 7 to 20 pairs of leaflets. Distinctive fruit is a narrow pod.
Habitat: Grasslands, sandy soils, deserts.
Comments: Wood is an excellent source of firewood, charcoal and fence posts. Named for its sweet seeds that Native Indians used in cakes and fermented drinks.

CALTROP FAMILY

Family of shrubs, herbs and trees found in hot climates.

CREOSOTE BUSH
Larrea tridentata
Size: To 10 ft. (3 m)
Description: One of the most common desert shrubs, it is told by its twisted, grayish stems and sparse foliage. Small yellow flowers (.5 in./1 cm) bloom throughout the year.
Habitat: Well drained soils in deserts to elevations of 5,000 ft. (1,500 m).
Comments: The plant exudes a pungent creosote odor following desert rains.

BUCKTHORNS

Family of woody shrubs and trees with over 700 species worldwide.

BLUEBLOSSOM
Ceanothus thyrsiflorus
Size: To 20 ft. (6 m)
Description: Shrub or small tree with branching clusters of showy, blue flowers. Green bark reddens with age.
Habitat: Coastal mountains, chaparral, mixed forests, roadsides.
Comments: Flowers are fragrant and reminiscent of lilacs.

BUCKEYES

Named for their dark-brown seeds that each have a light 'eye' spot.

CALIFORNIA BUCKEYE
Aesculus californica
Size: To 25 ft. (7.6 m)
Description: Shrub or small tree. Leaves have 5 to 7 pointed leaflets. Pinkish flowers bloom in erect clusters in late spring. Fruits have 1 or 2 seeds.
Habitat: Moist soils, canyons, chaparral, woodlands.
Comments: Seeds are poisonous and flower nectar is believed to kill bees.

HEATHS

Family of trees, shrubs and flowering plants that grow in acidic soils.

PACIFIC MADRONE
Arbutus menziesii
Size: To 80 ft. (24 m)
Description: Tree with smooth, red-brown branches and glossy, evergreen leaves. Clusters of white flowers bloom in spring and are succeeded by red-orange berries that often persist into winter.
Habitat: Moist and rocky soils, mixed woodlands.
Comments: The reddish outer bark regularly peels off in thin sections, exposing the smooth green inner bark that gradually darkens with age.

COMMON MANZANITA
Arctostaphylos manzanita
Size: 10-20 ft. (3-6 m)
Description: Shrub or small tree with grotesquely twisted trunk(s) and branches. Bark is reddish and smooth; leaves are thick and finely-haired. Urn-shaped pink flowers bloom in early spring and are succeeded by small berry-like fruits.
Habitat: Chaparral, foothills, dry rocky slopes in northern California.
Comments: Berries are a valuable food source for wildlife. *Manzanita* is Spanish for 'small apples.'

COMPOSITES

This huge family of plants includes over 13,000 species worldwide.

COYOTE BRUSH
Baccharis pitularis
Size: 10-15 ft. (3-5 m)
Description: Wiry evergreen shrub or small branching tree. Coarsely toothed, dull gray-green leaves grow alternately. Whitish-green flowers bloom in tight clusters and are succeeded by 'hairy' seeds.
Habitat: Chaparral, foothills.
Comments: Very common in coastal scrub areas, often in association with blueblossom and poison oak.

PALMS, YUCCAS AND CACTI

These evergreens are common in the warmer regions of California. They differ from other trees by having leaves with parallel veins and trunks that lack growth rings. Most have been introduced from the tropics.

CALIFORNIA FAN PALM
Washingtonia filifera
Size: 20-60 ft. (6-18 m)
Description: Told at a glance by its crown of large, fan-shaped leaves and the shaggy sack of dead leaves hanging beneath it.
Habitat: Moist soils.
Comments: Native to southeast California, it has been widely introduced elsewhere.

DATE PALM
Phoenix dactylifera
Size: To 75 ft. (23 m)
Description: Distinguished by its stout trunk and crown of ascending palm leaves. Trunk is roughened by the vestiges of dead leaves. Large clusters of small yellow flowers are succeeded by pulpy fruits.
Habitat: Moist soils.
Comments: A common non-native ornamental.

CANARY PALM
Phoenix canariensis
Size: To 50 ft. (15 m)
Description: Tree with stout, straight trunk and enormous, feathery, evergreen leaves that grow to 23 ft. (7 m) long.
Habitat: Moist soils throughout southern California.
Comments: Introduced over a century ago, it is commonly planted along streets.

COCONUT PALM
Cocos nucifera
Size: To 100 ft. (30 m)
Description: This classic desert-island palm is told by its smooth, often curved, trunk and large crown of feathery leaves. The familiar fruit is a fibrous nut 10-12 in. (25-30 cm) long.
Habitat: Most soils.
Comments: A widespread non-native species.

MOHAVE YUCCA
Yucca schidigera
Size. 10-16 ft. (3-4.8 m)
Description: Tree or shrub with upright branches and prominent, dagger-like leaves. White spring flower clusters are succeeded by cylindrical fruits.
Habitat: Found on dry soils at elevations to 5,000 ft. (1,500 m).
Comments: Native Indians obtained food, soap, blankets and ropes from this plant.

JOSHUA-TREE
Yucca brevifolia
Size: 15-30 ft. (4.5-9 m)
Description: A many-branched tree with terminal tufts of short, stiff, dagger-like leaves 6-10 in. (15-25 cm) long. Clusters of yellow tubular flowers bloom March-May and are succeeded by oblong fruits 2-4 in. (5-10 cm) long.
Habitat: Mohave desert.
Comments: Tree is a home for woodpeckers and fruit is a valuable source of food for desert wildlife. Joshua Tree National Park encompasses the largest stands of Joshua trees in the world.

TEDDYBEAR CHOLLA
Opuntia bigelovii
Size: 3-9 ft. (.9-2.7 m)
Description: A small, fuzzy-looking tree with branches covered with numerous inch-long, barbed spines. Pink flowers bloom at branch tips in summer and are succeeded by green, pear-shaped fruits.
Habitat: Dry, open areas in deserts.
Comments: This cute-sounding plant is anything but cuddly; the sharp spines easily penetrate skin and are extremely difficult to remove.

CHAINFRUIT CHOLLA
Opuntia fulgida
Size: To 15 ft. (4.5 m)
Description: Very spiny tree or shrub with a short trunk and numerous stout, jointed branches. Pinkish flowers bloom in spring and summer months and are succeeded by greenish, pear-shaped fruits.
Habitat: Desert plains and gentle slopes between 1,000-4,000 ft. (304-1,219 m).
Comments: Also called the jumping cholla, its fruits grow in hanging clusters and may remain attached for several years.

WHAT ARE WILDFLOWERS?

Wildflowers are soft-stemmed flowering plants, smaller than trees or shrubs, that grow anew each year. Some regenerate annually from the same root-stock (perennials), while others grow from seeds and last a single season (annuals). Most have flowering stems bearing colorful blossoms which ripen into fruits as the growing season progresses. The flowering stem typically grows upright, but may be climbing, creeping or trailing. Wildflowers range from weeds and reeds to roses and buttercups and are found almost everywhere. From the cracks in sidewalks to mountain meadows, wildflowers are abundant and widespread throughout California.

N.B. – *This section covers wildflowers and includes some shrubs that are conspicuous when in bloom.*

The species in this section have been grouped according to color rather than family in order to facilitate field identification. The color groups used are:

- White
- Yellow, Orange and Green
- Red and Pink
- Blue and Purple

HOW TO IDENTIFY WILDFLOWERS

After noting color, examine the shape of the flower heads. Are they daisy-like, bell-shaped, or odd in appearance? How are they arranged on the plant? Do they occur singly or in clusters? Are the flower heads upright or drooping? Pay close attention to the leaves and how they are arranged on the stem. Refer to the illustrations and text to confirm its size, habitat and blooming period.

N.B. – *The blooming periods of flowers can vary depending on latitude, elevation and the weather. The dates given are meant to serve as general guidelines only.*

Remember that flowers are wildlife and should be treated as such. Many species have been seriously depleted due to loss of habitat and overpicking. In many areas, once-abundant species are now rare. Bring along a sketch-book and camera to record the flowers you see instead of picking them. This will help ensure there are more blossoms for you and others to enjoy next year.

FLOWER STRUCTURE

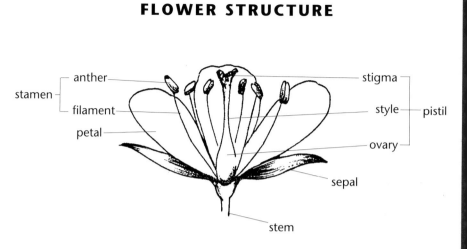

stamen { anther, filament

petal

stigma, style } pistil

ovary

sepal

stem

FLOWER SHAPES

Bell

Trumpet

Cross

Tubular

Iris

Pea-shaped

Two-lipped

Ray Flower

WHITE FLOWERS

WHITE TRILLIUM
Trillium ovatum
Size: To 16 in. (40 cm)
Description: White, 3-petalled flower is framed by a whorl of 3 broad leaves. Blooms February-June.
Habitat: Forest floors, stream banks in northern and central California.
Comments: Arrives with the robin in spring, it is also referred to as western wake robin.

FRAGRANT WATERLILY
Nymphaea odorata
Size: To 6 in. (15 cm)
Description: Common aquatic plant is distinguished by its large, many-rayed, white to pinkish, yellow-centered flowers. Round leafpads are notched at their base. Blooms nearly year-round.
Habitat: Ponds, lakes, streams.
Comments: This floating plant is rooted to the bottom and usually grows in water less than 8 ft. (2.4 m) deep.

WHITE VIRGIN'S BOWER
Clematis ligusticifolia
Size: Vine to 10 ft. (3 m)
Description: Vine covered with numerous beautiful cream flowers. Opposite leaves have 5 to 7 toothed leaflets. Blooms June-September.
Habitat: Canyons, gullies, chaparral, deserts.
Comments: Crushed leaves have a peppery aroma.

BINDWEED
Convolvulus arvensis
Size: To 3 ft. (90 cm)
Description: A twining plant with beautiful, white to pinkish funnel-shaped flowers. Blooms May-October.
Habitat: Gardens, waste areas, fields, farmlands.
Comments: Regarded as a weed by many, it is very difficult to eradicate because of its deep roots. A member of the morning-glory family.

ELEGANT CAMAS
Zigadenus elegans
Size: To 28 in. (70 cm)
Description: Told by grass-like leaves and branching cluster of white, lily-like flowers that bloom during summer months.
Habitat: Grassy slopes, mountain meadows, open forests.
Comments: Its bulb and leaves are very poisonous and can induce coma in humans and livestock.

ENGLISH DAISY
Bellis perennis
Size: To 8 in. (20 cm)
Description: Slender, leafless stalk supports a single, yellow-centered white flower with numerous rays. Basal leaves are rounded. Blooms March-September.
Habitat: Fields, waste areas, roadsides.
Comments: A common lawn weed introduced from Europe.

COMMON ICE PLANT
Mesembryanthemum crystallinum
Size: Stems 8-24 in. (20-60 cm)
Description: A creeping plant with beaded, glistening stems. Showy white or pinkish flowers bloom April-October.
Habitat: Sandy soils in coastal and desert regions in California.
Comments: The flowers open fully only in direct sunlight.

COW PARSNIP
Heracleum lanatum
Size: To 10 ft. (3 m)
Description: A large, conspicuous plant. Deeply-lobed leaves grow along the length of its thick, hollow stem. Dense, flattened clusters of creamy white flowers bloom February-September, depending on location.
Habitat: Very common in moist fields and woods.
Comments: Though non-poisonous, it resembles similar plants, like the water hemlock (*Cicuta maculata*), which are deadly.

PACIFIC DOGWOOD
Cornus nuttallii
Size: To 65 ft. (20 m)
Description: Typically a shrub or small tree bearing numerous large white or pinkish flowers. Small greenish flowers grow within the showy petal-like bracts.
Blooms April-June. Flowers are succeeded by red berries in fall.
Habitat: Undergrowth of dense forests to 6,000 ft. (1,800 m).
Comments: Dogwoods are widely planted as ornamentals and are prized for their hard wood.

WHITE CLOVER
Trifolium repens
Size: Stalks 4-24 in. (10-60 cm) long
Description: Long-stemmed, dark green leaves have 3 oval leaflets and grow densely along creeping, mat-forming stems. Rounded white flowers bloom April-September.
Habitat: Common in fields, lawns and waste areas.
Comments: An excellent nectar producer, it is a favorite of bees. Red and pink clovers are also found in California.

DESERT LILY
Hesperocallis undulata
Size: To 6 ft. (1.8 m)
Description: Large, funnel-shaped white flowers are unmistakable. Narrow leaves have wavy edges. Blooms March-May.
Habitat: Sandy soils in southeastern California.
Comments: Easily spotted when driving through the desert region.

WHITE SWEET CLOVER
Melilotus alba
Size: 2-10 ft. (.6-3 m)
Description: Tall leafy plant with long spikes of tiny, white, pea-shaped flowers. Blooms May-October.
Habitat: Roadsides, waste areas, fields.
Comments: Very common. Flowers have the scent of hay.

ARROWHEAD
Sagittaria latifolia
Size: To 3 ft. (90 cm)
Description: Small, white lily-like flowers bloom above arrow-shaped leaves during summer months.
Habitat: Ponds, slow streams, marshes, ditches.
Comments: The plant produces underground tubers that were an important food source for early settlers.

OUR LORD'S CANDLE
Yucca whipplei
Size: To 11 ft. (3.3 m)
Description: Stout, spiny stalk supports huge, elongate cluster of cream to white, bell-shaped flowers. Blooms March-May.
Habitat: Chaparral.
Comments: Often blooms by the hundreds on brushy slopes in southern California.

YARROW
Achillea millefolium
Size: To 39 in. (98 cm)
Description: A long, unbranched stem supports dense clusters of round, yellow-centered daisy-like flowers. Each flower has 4 to 6 white (occasionally pinkish) rays. The unusual fern-like leaves are a good field mark. Blooms March-October.
Habitat: Common in ditches, fields and waste areas.
Comments: An aromatic herb, it is also known as milfoil.

PHLOX
Phlox **spp.**
Size: To 20 in. (50 cm)
Description: Sprawling herbs or small shrubs with numerous showy, 5-lobed, yellow-centered flowers. Petals fold back from a narrow tube. Flowers range in color from pink and lavender to yellow and white, and several variants may be found within a small area. Blooms April-September.
Habitat: Dry soils in a variety of habitats.
Comments: About 12 species of phlox are found in California.

INDIAN PIPE
Monotropa uniflora
Size: To 12 in. (30 cm)
Description: Waxy, white plant has several stems supporting a single, nodding, cup-shaped, white to pinkish flower. The entire plant darkens in color with age.
Habitat: Deciduous woods and shady places in central and northern California.
Comments: It lacks the pigment chlorophyll necessary for photosynthesis and obtains nourishment from living and decaying plants.

BEACH STRAWBERRY
Fragaria chiloensis
Size: To 8 in. (20 cm)
Description: Mat-forming plant has coarsely-toothed, leathery leaves with three leaflets. Crisp white flowers bloom March-August and are succeeded in late summer by the familiar fruit.
Habitat: Open areas, forest margins, hillsides.
Comments: This plant commonly interbreeds with the domestic strawberry.

POISON OAK
Toxicodendron diversilobum
Size: To 13 ft. (3.9 m)
Description: An upright shrub or climbing vine with drooping leaves and white berries in loose clusters along the stem. Leaves have three rounded or oak-like leaflets. Small whitish flowers bloom in summer and are succeeded by hard, whitish berries. Plant is showy in fall when its leaves turn bright red.
Habitat: Shaded woods, chaparral, brushy slopes.
Comments: Contact with the leaves, stems or flowers can cause a severe rash. Washing affected area thoroughly with soap and water is recommended.

SOUTHWESTERN THORNAPPLE
Datura wrightii
Size: To 5 ft. (1.5 m)
Description: Large, white trumpet-shaped flowers arise from coarse, rank-smelling, gray-green foliage. Fragrant flowers bloom May-October, and are succeeded by round, prickly fruits.
Habitat: Sandy soil, gullies, woodlands.
Comments: Flowers bloom in evenings and wither in the morning. The plant is pollinated at night by sphinx moths. All parts of the plant are poisonous.

YELLOW, ORANGE & GREEN FLOWERS

SUBALPINE BUTTERCUP
Ranunculus eschscholtzii
Size: To 10 in. (25 cm)
Description: Shiny, yellow flower with five overlapping petals and smooth, oval leaves. Blooms June-August.
Habitat: Mountain meadows, rocky slopes, fields.
Comments: One of over 20 species of buttercup found in California.

TREE TOBACCO
Nicotiana glauca
Size: To 26 ft. (8 m)
Description: Shrub or small tree with open, spreading branches. Tubular flowers bloom at night in spreading clusters between April-November.
Habitat: Roadsides, disturbed areas, washes in central California.
Comments: Common along roadsides, it is one of 12 species of plants containing nicotine found in North America.

DESERT CANDLE
Caulanthus inflatus
Size: To 2 ft. (60 cm)
Description: Slender yellow-stemmed plant covered in small white or purplish flower. Blooms May-July.
Habitat: Deserts, dry slopes. Often associated with sagebrush.
Comments: Related to mustard plants.

GOLDFIELDS
Lasthenia californica
Size: To 10 in. (25 cm)
Description: Slender, reddish stems with opposite, narrow leaves support small yellow flowers. Blooms spring.
Habitat: Poor soils, open, dry areas.
Comments: When enough moisture is available, this flower literally blankets open areas with gold.

COMMON SUNFLOWER
Helianthus annuus
Size: To 13 ft. (3.9 m)
Description: Tall, leafy plant
with a branching stem supporting
numerous yellow, dark-centered
flowers. Blooms June-September.
Habitat: Roadsides, waste areas,
open fields.
Comments: Flowers follow the sun
across the sky each day.

DESERT PRICKLY PEAR CACTUS
Opuntia spp.
Size: Pads to 3 ft. (90 cm)
Description: A sprawling or erect cactus
with jointed, prickly pads. Red-centered,
yellow flowers bloom April-June.
Habitat: Deserts, rangeland, waste areas.
Comments: There are more than 20
species of prickly pear cactus in the U.S.
Both the fruit 'tuna' and the pads are
consumed by humans and wildlife.

GOLDENROD
Solidago canadensis
Size: To 5 ft. (1.5 m)
Description: Tall, leafy plant with
spreading, arched clusters of tiny
yellow flowers. Leaves are hairy with 3
distinct veins. Blooms May-September.
Habitat: Meadows, pastures,
open forests.
Comments: Widespread to the point
that it is considered a nuisance in some
areas.

BLAZING STAR
Mentzelia laevicaulis
Size: To 3 ft. (90 cm)
Description: Large, star-shaped, waxy
yellow flowers feature a central puff of
long stamens. Flowers bloom at the tips
of white, satiny stems June-September.
Habitat: Waste areas, roadsides,
deserts.
Comments: A member of the stick-
tight family, it has toothed leaves
covered with barbed hairs that cling
to fabric.

RABBITBRUSH
Chrysothamnus nauseosus
Size: 3-7 ft. (.9-2.1 m)
Description: Small shrub with wiry, hairy stems. Terminal clusters of small yellow flowers bloom August-October.
Habitat: Grasslands and dry areas mainly in the Great Basin region.
Comments: An important food source for jackrabbits and deer.

COMMON DANDELION
Taraxacum officinale
Size: To 20 in. (50 cm)
Description: Told by its elongate, toothed leaves and shaggy yellow flowers. Tufts of whitish, hairy seeds succeed the flowers and are dispersed by the wind.
Habitat: Grassy and waste areas.
Comments: The leaves are often used in salads and the blossoms for wine-making.

CREAMCUPS
Platystemon californicus
Size: To 12 in. (30 cm)
Description: Hairy plant with narrow, opposite leaves. Bowl-shaped, 6-petalled yellow flowers bloom atop slender stalks March-May.
Habitat: Moist meadows, fields, hillsides.
Comments: Grows in dense colonies and often covers entire fields.

ST. JOHN'S WORT
Hypericum perforatum
Size: To 3 ft. (90 cm)
Description: Branching, leafy stem supports a cluster of star-shaped yellow flowers, often with black dots near the tips. Blooms June-September.
Habitat: Pastures, roadsides, waste areas.
Comments: A troublesome weed very common throughout California. Can be poisonous to livestock. Plant extract is a popular herbal remedy.

CALIFORNIA POPPY
Eschscholzia californica
Size: To 2 ft. (60 cm)
Description: Distinguished by its delicate yellow-orange flowers and fern-like leaves. Blooms February-September.
Habitat: Open areas.
Comments: The flowers are light sensitive and close at night.

California's State Wildflower

SHRUBBY CINQUEFOIL
Potentilla fruticosa
Size: To 3 ft. (90 cm)
Description: Small, woody plant with reddish, shredding bark and yellow flowers. Toothed leaves have 3 or 5 lobes. Blooms June-August.
Habitat: Pastures, roadsides, hillsides, gardens, meadows.
Comments: Widely cultivated as an ornamental.

REDWOOD VIOLET
Viola sempervirens
Size: Stalks to 5 in. (13 cm)
Description: Creeping plant forms dense mats of leathery, heart-shaped leaves. Dark-centered, yellow flowers face outward
Habitat: Very common in moist forests, clearings and near streams at low to middle elevations.
Comments: Several other similar species of mauve, blue and white violets are found in California.

EVENING PRIMROSE
Oenothera spp.
Size: To 3 ft. (90 cm)
Description: Tall plant with long, slender leaves. Large, 4-petalled yellow flowers bloom June-September.
Habitat: Roadsides and grassy slopes from low to middle elevations.
Comments: As the common name suggests, the flowers open near the end of the day.

COMMON MONKEYFLOWER
Mimulus guttatus
Size: To 3 ft. (90 cm)
Description: Trumpet-shaped yellow flowers have dark-spotted, hairy throats. Oval leaves are coarsely toothed; lower leaves are stalked, upper ones are clasping. Flowers bloom in loose terminal clusters March-September.
Habitat: Wet areas, meadows, and ditches at most elevations.
Comments: Pink, purple, red and white monkey flowers are also found in California.

GREAT BASIN SAGEBRUSH
Artemisia tridentata
Size: 2-20 ft. (.6-6 m)
Description: Gray-green shrub or small tree with narrow, 3-toothed, wedge-shaped leaves. Inconspicuous yellowish flowers bloom at stem tips.
Habitat: Deserts, mountain slopes and plains in eastern California.
Comments: Plant emits an aromatic sage odor when handled. Important food source for deer, grouse and livestock. Coastal sagebrush (*Artemisia californica*), common along the south-west coast of California, has thin, grass-like leaves.

WOOLLY MULLEIN
Verbascum thapsus
Size: To 7 ft. (2.1 m)
Description: Tall leafy plant that tapers from a broad base to a slender spike of yellow flowers. Flowers bloom a few at a time throughout summer.
Habitat: Roadsides, fields and waste areas.
Comments: Gold miners used to make torches from these plants by dipping them in tallow.

TARWEED
Madia elegans
Size: To 4 ft. (1.2 m)
Description: Stem is hairy and sticky; leaves are long and narrow. Flower petals (rays) are toothed near the outer edge and maroon-colored near the base.
Habitat: Dry areas, along roadsides.
Comments: Named for its sticky stem, it is abundant throughout California. Also called common madia.

BARREL CACTUS
Ferocactus acanthodes
Size: 3-10 ft. (1-3 m)
Description: Yellowish flowers bloom atop this rounded cactus in spring.
Habitat: Dry hills, gravelly slopes.
Comments: Its succulent stem is able to absorb large amounts of water during short rainy spells. Spines help to reduce water loss by evaporation.

YELLOW SAND VERBENA
Abronia latifolia
Size: Stems 2-6 ft. (60-180 cm)
Description: Creeping plant has trumpet-shaped yellow flowers to 2 in. (5 cm) wide.
Habitat: Coastal dunes above the tideline.
Comments: The roots were once considered a delicacy by Native Americans.

YELLOW SALSIFY
Tragopogon dubius
Size: 15-30 in. (38-75 cm)
Description: Branching hollow stems have grass-like leaves. Pale yellow flowerhead is distinctive.
Habitat: Roadsides, waste areas.
Comments: The flowers are succeeded by seed-like fruits covered in feathery brown bristles.

COMMON CATTAIL
Typha latifolia
Size: To 10 ft. (3 m)
Description: Distinguished by its prominent club-like sheath of greenish flower spikes atop a long stalk. The flowers ripen into brownish tufts of hairy seeds in late summer.
Habitat: Common in marshes, ditches and along lakes and rivers.
Comments: Cattails provide a vital source of food and cover for water birds and wildlife.

STINGING NETTLE
Urtica gracilis
Size: To 10 ft. (3 m)
Description: Coarsely saw-toothed, opposite leaves have sharp prickles that eject an acidic stinging fluid (formic acid) on contact. Drooping spikes of green flowers bloom June-August.
Habitat: Shady thickets, meadows, waste areas, along creeks.
Comments: Common throughout California.

COMMON PLANTAIN
Plantago major
Size: To 20 in. (50 cm)
Description: Large, tough basal leaves are finely-toothed with deep longitudinal veins. Tiny greenish flowers bloom in a slender spike.
Habitat: Very common in lawns, gardens and waste areas.
Comments: An introduced weed widespread throughout the country.

RED & PINK FLOWERS

SKYROCKET
Ipomopsis aggregata
Size: To 7 ft. (2.1 m)
Description: Slender stems support clusters of bright red, tubular flowers resembling exploded fireworks. Blooms May-September.
Habitat: Open woodlands, dry hillsides.
Comments: Foliage has a skunky odor.

FIREWEED
Chamerion angustifolium
Size: To 7 ft. (2.1 m)
Description: Distinguished by a long conical spike of bright pink, four-petalled flowers. Blooms June-September.
Habitat: Very common in open woodlands, clearings and burned-out areas.
Comments: Often grows in dense colonies.

TWINFLOWER
Linnaea borealis
Size: To 4 in. (10 cm)
Description: Trailing shrub has rounded, opposite, evergreen leaves. Slender stems support nodding pairs of pink, bell-shaped flowers. Blooms May-July.
Habitat: Moist woods.
Comments: Flowers are sweetly fragrant.

INDIAN PAINTBRUSH
Castilleja spp.
Size: To 3 ft. (90 cm)
Description: Ragged, red wildflower often grows in dense colonies. Blooms May-September.
Habitat: Woodlands and mountain meadows.
Comments: Related to snapdragons, paintbrushes occur in a variety of colors. 33 species occur in California.

BEAVERTAIL CACTUS
Opuntia basilaris
Size: Pads to 18 in. (45 cm)
Description: Jointed, flattened cactus segments grow in clumps. Showy pink flowers bloom April-June.
Habitat: Deserts, rocky slopes.
Comments: Widely planted as an ornamental in southern California.

FAREWELL-TO-SPRING
Clarkia amoena
Size: To 3 ft. (90 cm)
Description: Slender, branching stem with showy, pinkish, poppy-like flowers. Petals often have a central blotch of maroon. Blooms June-August.
Habitat: Open woods and grassy slopes in coastal northern California.
Comments: Flowers close at night and re-open in the morning.

FRINGE CUPS
Tellima grandiflora
Size: To 31 in. (78 cm)
Description: Pinkish to white, cup-shaped, fringed flowers grow along slender stalks rising from a leafy base. Blooms May-July.
Habitat: Moist, shaded woodlands in northern California.
Comments: Abundant along the coast.

REDWOOD SORREL
Oxalis oregana
Size: To 7 in. (18 cm)
Description: Tiny pink flowers bloom amidst a carpet of shamrock-shaped leaves from April-September. Leaflets often have a pale blotch down their middle.
Habitat: Moist, shaded woods.
Comments: Abundant in the understorey of redwood forests.

CANADA THISTLE
Cirsium arvense
Size: To 5 ft. (1.5 m)
Description: Tall plant with scalloped, prickly leaves and puffy pink flowers. Blooms May-October.
Habitat: Fields, ditches, waste areas.
Comments: This ubiquitous weed is common throughout North America, Asia and Europe. Flowers are sweet-smelling and rich in nectar.

WOODS' ROSE
Rosa woodsii
Size: To 5 ft. (1.5 m)
Description: A prickly shrub with broad, pink, 5-petalled, sweet-smelling flowers. Blooms April-September.
Habitat: Open areas and woodlands.
Comments: Flowers are succeeded by fruits called hips that are rich in vitamin C and used in teas. At least eight other species of wild rose occur in California.

WILD GINGER
Asarum caudatum
Size: Stems to 6 in. (15 cm) long
Description: Creeping plant has unusual purplish-brown flowers and large, glossy heart-shaped leaves.
Habitat: Moist woodlands.
Comments: The crushed leaves and rootstocks smell like ginger. The flowers are often well hidden beneath the leaves. Often carpets large areas.

FOXGLOVE
Digitalis purpurea
Size: To 7 ft. (2.1 m)
Description: Showy plant with prominent cluster of nodding lavender flowers. Blooms June-July.
Habitat: Disturbed areas, wooded slopes, roadsides. Especially abundant near coast.
Comments: An extract from this plant is the heart stimulant, digitalis.

CALIFORNIA RHODODENDRON
Rhododendron macrophyllum
Size: To 25 ft. (7.6 m)
Description: Handsome flowering shrub or small tree with broad clusters of white to pink, trumpet-shaped flowers. Large, leathery evergreen leaves have edges rolled under. Blooms April-August.
Habitat: Moist, shaded areas in forests below 4,000 ft. (1,220 m).
Comments: Associated with pines, redwoods and Douglas-fir.

CARDINAL FLOWER
Lobelia cardinalis
Size: To 3 ft. (90 cm)
Description: Plant with spike of striking red, tubular flowers. Blooms June-October.
Habitat: Wet, open areas, moist woods in southern California.
Comments: Also called scarlet lobelia, its flowers are a favorite of humming-birds.

RED COLUMBINE
Aquilegia formosa
Size: To 3 ft. (90 cm)
Description: Stunning red-orange flower head with tall spurs is unmistakable. Blooms May-August.
Habitat: Open woods, meadows, glades.
Comments: Blue and white columbines are also found in California.

SHOOTING STAR
Dodecatheon pulchellum
Size: To 2 ft. (60 cm)
Description: Graceful plant with drooping, dart-like reddish flowers with inverted petals exposing yellow stamen tube. Blooms May-August.
Habitat: Moist soils in meadows, fields and open woodlands.
Comments: Several similar species are found in California. Related to primroses and cyclamens.

PINE DROPS
Pterospora andromedea
Size: To 3 ft. (90 cm)
Description: Slender, hairy, red-brown stalks covered with small, yellowish egg-shaped flowers.
Habitat: Coniferous forests.
Comments: It is a root parasite of conifers. Commonly associated with ponderosa pine.

COMMON FLEABANE
Erigeron philadelphicus
Size: To 3 ft. (90 cm)
Description: Narrow leaves clasp the stem and are densely clustered at the plant base. Pink to white ray flowers bloom in loose clusters June-August.
Habitat: Moist meadows, open woods.
Comments: One of several fleabanes found in Alaska. The plants were once hung in houses to keep fleas away. Similar to asters, the flower rays are narrower and more numerous.

DESERT GLOBEMALLOW
Sphaeralcea ambigua
Size: To 40 in. (1 m)
Description: Hairy, branching plant with striking red-orange flowers. Leaves are three-lobed and coarsely toothed. Blooms March-June.
Habitat: Deserts.
Comments: Genus name refers to the spherical fruit that succeeds the flowers.

STRIPED CORAL ROOT
Corallorhiza striata
Size: To 20 in. (50 cm)
Description: Medium-sized plant with a spire of dark-striped flowers.
Habitat: Moist woodlands.
Comments: It lacks chlorophyll and obtains food by absorbing nutrients from the organic matter it grows in.

CALIFORNIA FUCHSIA
Epilobium canum
Size: To 3 ft. (90 cm)
Description: Bushy, gray-green plant with a profusion of red, tubular flowers. Blooms August-October.
Habitat: Dry slopes from sea level to upper mountain elevations.
Comments: This late-bloomer is easily spotted in autumn. An important food source for hummingbirds.

BITTERROOT
Lewisia rediviva
Size: To 2 in. (5 cm)
Description: Ground-hugging plant with beautiful pinkish flowers. Blooms March-June.
Habitat: Barren, dry ground, gravelly slopes and rocky areas.
Comments: Associated with sagebrush and pines. Also called sandrose.

PIPSISSEWA
Chimaphila umbellata
Size: To 10 in. (25 cm)
Description: Leathery, evergreen leaves are coarsely-toothed and whorled around the stem. Small, saucer-shaped, waxy pink flowers bloom in nodding clusters of 3-10 between June-August.
Habitat: Found in cool, moist coniferous forests.
Comments: Leaves were once used as a tea substitute by early settlers.

BLUE & PURPLE FLOWERS

ELEGANT BRODIAEA
Brodiaea elegans
Size: To 20 in. (50 cm)
Description: Leafless stalk supports several funnel-shaped, blue-purple flowers that bloom April-July.
Habitat: Dry soils, grasslands.
Comments: 37 species of brodiaea are found in the western states.

DESERT SAND VERBENA
Abronia villosa
Size: To 10 in. (25 cm)
Description: Small, sticky creeping plants with dense clusters of tiny lavender flowers. Opposite leaves have wavy edges. Blooms February-October.
Habitat: Deserts in sandy soil.
Comments: Plants often form a carpet covering miles of open desert following rains.

SHOWY MILKWEED
Asclepias speciosa
Size: To 4 ft. (1.2 m)
Description: Red-purplish, horned flowers bloom in tight clusters May-August. Large, fleshy leaves are finely-haired. In autumn, long seed pods split open to release thousands of conspicuous, long-plumed seeds.
Habitat: Dry soils in waste areas and ditches, open forests.
Comments: Both the leaves and stem secrete a sticky fluid to protect the flowers from crawling insects.

PURPLE LOOSESTRIFE
Lythrum salicaria
Size: To 7 ft. (2.1 m)
Description: Square stems have clasping lance-shaped leaves. Brilliant purplish flowers bloom in a long spike.
Habitat: Marshes
Comments: Introduced from Europe in the 1880s, this plant has become an invasive weed and outcompetes many native plants for survival.

ASTER
Aster spp.
Size: To 12 in. (30 cm)
Description: Narrow leaves grow alternately along stem. Purple, yellow-centered starburst flowers.
Habitat: Woodlands, moist meadows, mountain hillsides.
Comments: One of several species of aster found in California. All have similar starburst flower heads.

COMMON CAMAS
Camassia quamash
Size: To 28 in. (70 cm)
Description: Striking blue, star-shaped flowers bloom April-June. Leaves are narrow and grass-like.
Habitat: Moist soils in meadows and open areas.
Comments: Often covers entire meadows. Plant bulbs were food for Native Americans.

MINIATURE LUPINE
Lupinus bicolor
Size: To 14 in. (36 cm)
Description: Branching, hairy
plant with bluish flowers arranged
in whorls around the stem. Blooms
March-May. Note star shaped leaves.
Habitat: Open slopes, grassy areas.
Comments: Often associated with the
California poppy, it grows in dense
colonies and may blanket entire fields.

BLUEBELLS
Mertensia spp.
Size: To 5 ft. (1.5 m)
Description: Leaves grow along length
of branching stem. Clusters of bell-
shaped blue, nodding flowers bloom in
open clusters.
Habitat: Meadows, beaches and
woodlands.
Comments: Flowers are occasionally
pink or white. Also known as lungwort

FRINGED GENTIAN
Gentianopsis detonsa
Size: To 16 in. (40 cm)
Description: Beautiful blue-violet,
bell-shaped flowers have delicately
fringed edges. Blooms in summer.
Habitat: Moist areas in the foothills
and mountains.
Comments: Often cultivated as an
ornamental.

CHICORY
Cichorium intybus
Size: To 6 ft. (1.8 m)
Description: Wheel-shaped, pale
blue flowers bloom atop wiry
branching stems April-October.
Habitat: Fields, roadsides, waste
areas.
Comments: The roots can be
roasted and used as a coffee substitute. The leaves are also edible. The
cultivated Endive is a closely related
species.

OYSTERPLANT
Tragopogon porrifolius
Size: To 4 ft. (1.2 m)
Description: Purple flowerhead blooms atop a swollen stem during summer.
Habitat: Fields, waste areas.
Comments: The palnt root has the flavor of oysters when cooked. Its leaves are also edible. Also known as salisify.

WILD BLUE FLAX
Linum perenne
Size: To 31 in. (78 cm)
Description: Delicate sky-blue, yellow-centered flowers bloom atop slender, wiry stems MarchSeptember.
Habitat: Prairies, meadows, hillsides.
Comments: The tough stems were used by Native Indians to make cords.

WILD TEASEL
Dipsacus fullonum
Size: To 7 ft. (2.1 m)
Description: Prickly plant with a spikey purple flowerhead. Grass-like, erect leaves are also prickly on their undersides. Blooms April-September.
Habitat: Moist soils, fields, open woodlands.
Comments: Related to the garden variety pincushions.

AMERICAN VETCH
Vicia americana
Size: To 4 ft. (1.2 m) long
Description: A climbing vine with clusters of 4-10 purplish, pea-shaped flowers. Flowers turn blue as they age. Blooms April-July.
Habitat: Open woodlands, roadsides.
Comments: Similar to a number of wild pea plants.

MISSION BELLS
Fritillaria affinis
Size: To 4 ft. (1.2 m)
Description: Dark purple-brown, nodding, bell-shaped flowers with bright yellow anthers. Narrow leaves grow in whorls around the stem.
Habitat: Open woods, grassy areas.
Comments: Named by the early Spanish priests who founded the first missions.

MONKSHOOD
Aconitum columbianum
Size: To 7 ft. (2.1 m)
Description: A leafy plant with deep blue flowers resembling a monk's habit. Blooms June-September.
Habitat: Mountain meadows, moist woods.
Comments: Related species have medicinal uses, and many are poisonous.

BABY BLUE EYES
Nemophila menziesii
Size: To 12 in. (30 cm)
Description: Low, mat-forming plant with pale blue, 5-petalled flowers. Petals are typically paler near the base and spotted with black dots. Blooms February-June.
Habitat: Open woods, meadows.
Comments: A well-known, popular wildflower that is sold commercially.

BLUE-EYED GRASS
Sisyrinchium angustifolium
Size: To 20 in. (50 cm)
Description: Slender stems support one or more delicate, 6-petalled, star-shaped blue-violet flowers. Blooms March-September.
Habitat: Moist areas in woodlands and meadows.
Comments: Its yellow cousin, golden-eyed grass, is also found in California.

CALIFORNIA REGIONS

Eureka

1

2

Sacramento

San Francisco

3

4

5

6

Bakersfield

8

7

Los Angeles

San Diego

1 NORTH COAST

2 SHASTA CASCADE

3 BAY AREA DELTA

4 CENTRAL VALLEY

5 SIERRA NEVADA

6 CENTRAL COAST

7 SOUTH COAST

8 DESERT

NATURAL ATTRACTIONS & SANCTUARIES

Californians have dedicated hundreds of parks, sanctuaries and museums to preserve and showcase the state's natural beauty. This precious heritage provides unsurpassed educational and recreational benefits for residents and tourists alike.

We have divided California into 8 regions that generally reflect the biodiversity in different parts of the state.

1 NORTH COAST

Stretching for over 300 miles, the North Coast is characterized by primeval forests of towering redwoods and a rugged, often fog-shrouded coast. This land's raw beauty appeals to nature lovers and casual travellers who come to explore old growth forests, magnificent shorelines, coastal tidepools and seek out herds of grazing elk.

2 SHASTA CASCADE

This region is less commercialized than most of California and offers visitors some of the best back-country adventuring the state has to offer. The scenery in the north is dominated by Mount Shasta, a huge, dormant volcano visible for over 100 miles. The Lassen Volcanic National Park provides visitors with a glimpse of current volcanic activity in its hot pools and bubbling mudpots.

3 BAY AREA DELTA

A richly endowed region, the Bay Area Delta is known for its vast tidal marshes, rich farmland and prominent sanctuaries and museums. The region's expansive wetlands attract an abundance of migrating birds and serve as a vital nursery for fish fry and shellfish.

4 CENTRAL VALLEY

This region is a major off-ramp of the Pacific flyway, an aerial highway used by millions of birds during migrations. While the majority of birds merely stop to refuel, many stay to nest. This region is also the most productive farming area in the state and has thousands of miles of waterways.

5 SIERRA NEVADA

The Sierra Nevada Mountains are home to some of California's greatest natural treasures. Giant sequoias, the largest living trees, grace several state and national parks. Lake Tahoe is one of the largest and deepest alpine lakes on earth. Yosemite's breathtaking waterfalls and pristine wilderness attract millions of visitors each year from around the world.

6 CENTRAL COAST

This region encompasses what many believe to be the most spectacular coastal area of California. Major attractions include battling bull elephant seals, Butterfly Town U.S.A., the world-renowned Monterey Bay Aquarium and the extensive coastal dune systems in the south.

7 SOUTH COAST

It is not surprising that this heavily-populated region is most famous for its man-made sanctuaries and museums. Sea World, the San Diego Zoo, the Museum of La Brea Discoveries and the San Diego Wild Animal Park are all top attractions. For the adventurous, a trip to the remote Channel Islands sanctuary provides excellent wildlife viewing opportunities.

8 DESERT

The expansive desert region is home to a variety of unusual plants and animals adapted to the hot, dry climate. Although it includes the hottest place in the western hemisphere – Death Valley – California's deserts also feature a number of lush habitats that harbor a diversity of wildlife.

NORTH COAST

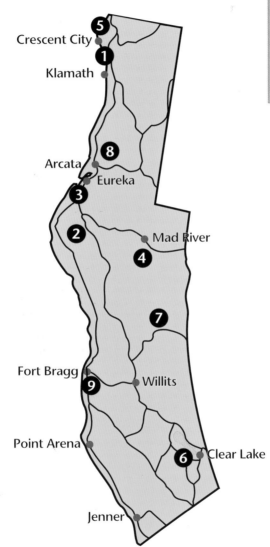

Crescent City

Klamath

Arcata

Eureka

Mad River

Fort Bragg

Willits

Point Arena

Clear Lake

Jenner

Parks/Wildlife Areas

❶ REDWOOD NATIONAL PARK

This 110,000-acre park features vast groves of coastal redwoods (including the world's tallest trees), salt marshes, sandy beaches, rivers and lakes, and about 30 miles of coastline. Reservations required for camp-grounds May-September. Stop at Redwood Information Center in Orick to get a free permit to drive to the redwood grove featuring the world's first-, third- and fifth-tallest trees.
Location: Crescent City
Phone: (707) 464-6101

❷ HUMBOLDT REDWOODS STATE PARK

The famous Avenue of the Giants – an unforgettable 33-mile drive through some of the tallest trees on earth – traverses the length of this 51,000-acre park. Features include Founder's Grove and the 10,000-acre Rockefeller Forest. Numerous parking areas, picnic sites and nature trails.
Location: South of Eureka
Phone: (707) 946-2409

❸ HUMBOLDT BAY NATIONAL WILDLIFE REFUGE

Huge eelgrass beds, tidal flats, mud-flats and grasslands. Major staging area for black brant geese (up to 40,000 at a time) in spring and fall.
Location: South of Eureka
Phone: (707) 733-5406

❹ RUTH LAKE

Bald eagles, herons, deer and otters are just a few of the resident species at this out-of-the-way refuge. Considered a birding hotspot, it is one of the region's best kept secrets.
Location: South of Mad River
Phone: (707) 574-6332

❺ LAKE EARL WILDLIFE AREA

Fresh- and saltwater marshes surrounded by groves of alder and spruce provide staging areas for 100,000 migratory waterfowl.
Location: North of Crescent City
Phone: (707) 464-2523

❻ CLEAR LAKE STATE PARK

California's second-largest freshwater lake is a popular resort and fishing area. Spring wildflower displays and fall colors are two annual highlights. Excellent birding year round with up to half a million wintering birds.
Location: Near Clear Lake
Phone: (707) 279-4293

❼ MENDOCINO NATIONAL FOREST

More than 1,000,000 acres of mountainous and rolling terrain along California's north coast.
Location: Northeast of Willits
Phone: (530) 934-3316

Museums/Sanctuaries

❽ HUMBOLDT STATE UNIVERSITY NATURAL HISTORY MUSEUM

Exhibits of more than 2,000 species of ancient and living plants and animals. Collection of fossils includes saber-toothed cats, a *Tyrannosaurus rex* skull and jaws of a 70-foot great white shark.
Location: Arcata
Phone: (707) 826-4479

❾ MENDOCINO COAST BOTANICAL GARDENS

Nature trails and two miles of coastal trails wind through 47 acres of gardens, woods and meadows.
Location: Near Fort Bragg
Phone: (707) 964-4352

SHASTA CASCADE

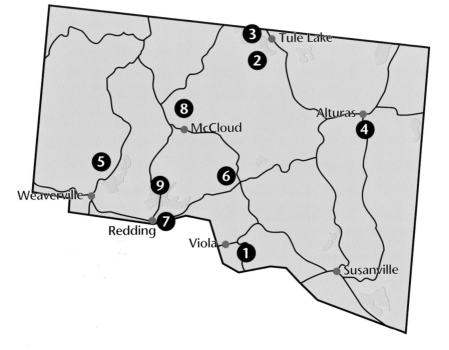

3 Tule Lake

2

8
McCloud

Alturas
4

5

Weaverville

9

6

Redding **7**

Viola **1**

Susanville

Parks/Wildlife Areas

❶ LASSEN VOLCANIC NATIONAL PARK

Features 100,000 acres of alpine wilderness and moe than 50 lakes. Mt. Lassen, the world's largest plug volcano, was active earlier this century, erupting 300 times between 1914-1922. Attractions include boiling lakes, bubbling mud pools, fumaroles and sulphur vents. Paths wind around and over some fascinating thermal areas.
Location: East of Viola
Phone: (530) 595-4444

❷ LAVA BEDS NATIONAL MONUMENT

Lava tube caves, cinder cones and lava flows are just a few of the attractions that can be explored at this dormant volcano.
Location: Tulelake
Phone: (530) 667-8100

❸ KLAMATH BASIN NATIONAL WILDLIFE REFUGES

Six refuges of 86,000 acres encompass a variety of habitats including wetlands, marshes, farmlands and uplands. Fall migrations bring up to two million birds, primarily geese and ducks. Bald eagles are a common winter visitor.
Location: Near Tulelake
Phone: (530) 667-2231

❹ MODOC NATIONAL WILDLIFE REFUGE

A 6,200 acre refuge with numerous lakes, ponds, streams, marshes and farmland.
Location: Alturas
Phone: (530) 233-3572

❺ SHASTA-TRINITY NATIONAL FOREST

2.1 million-acre forest features high mountains (Mt. Shasta 14,161 ft.), rolling hills, river valleys, 131 lakes and numerous rivers and streams. Contains California's second largest wilderness area.
Location: Weaverville
Phone: (530) 226-2500

❻ McARTHUR-BURNEY FALLS MEMORIAL STATE PARK

Highlight is a 129-ft. waterfall that Teddy Roosevelt called the eighth wonder of the world. 100 million gallons of water rush over the falls each day.
Location: Northeast of Redding
Phone: (530) 335-2777

Museums/Sanctuaries

❼ CARTER HOUSE NATURAL SCIENCE MUSEUM

Features exhibits on local natural history and science.
Location: Redding
Phone: (530) 243-5457

❽ MOUNT SHASTA HATCHERY

The oldest fish hatchery in western North America features pools with more than 100,000 trout. Trout viewing and feeding.
Location: Mt. Shasta
Phone: (530) 926-2215

❾ LAKE SHASTA CAVERNS

Lake Shasta boasts 370 miles of shoreline and a series of spectacular caverns where visitors can view stalactites, stalagmites and raw crystal formations.
Location: Lake Shasta
Phone: (530) 238-2341

BAY AREA DELTA

Calistoga

Suisun City
4

Vallejo
1
9

Stinson Beach 10

3

8
6
7 Oakland

San Francisco

5

Half Moon Bay
2 Fremont

San Jose

Parks/Wildlife Areas

❶ POINT REYES NATIONAL SEASHORE

Meadows, bays, streams, lagoons, beaches and more than 800 flowering plants make this 73,000-acre sanctuary an exceptional birding area. Point Reyes Bird Sanctuary is located within the National Seashore.
Location: Point Reyes Station
Phone: (415) 464-5100

❷ SAN FRANCISCO BAY NATIONAL WILDLIFE REFUGE

20,000 acres of grassy uplands, mudflats, marshlands and tidal flats support a diversity of bird life.
Location: Near Fremont
Phone: (510) 792-0222

❸ MUIR WOODS NATIONAL MONUMENT

One of the most majestic and accessible redwood groves has trees up to 250 ft. tall (76 m) and more than 1,000 years old.
Location: North of San Francisco
Phone: (415) 388-2595

❹ GRIZZLY ISLAND WILDLIFE AREA

The largest estuarine marsh in the U.S. provides excellent birding and nature study opportunities.
Location: Near Suisun City
Phone: (707) 425-3828

❺ FITZGERALD MARINE RESERVE

Observe all varieties of seashore life up close in California's largest natural tidal pools.
Location: Half Moon Bay
Phone: (415) 363-4020

Museums/Sanctuaries

❻ OAKLAND MUSEUM

A complex of galleries and gardens feature dramatic exhibits on native plants and animals that provide an excellent introduction to the natural history of California.
Location: Oakland
Phone: (510) 238-2200

❼ CALIFORNIA ACADEMY OF SCIENCES

The oldest science institution in the western U.S. is a museum, aquarium and planetarium rolled into one. Innovative exhibits highlight native wildlife and plants, evolution, human cultures and astronomy.
Location: San Francisco
Phone: (415) 321-8000

❽ STRYBING ARBORETUM AND BOTANICAL GARDEN

More than 5,000 species of plants on 70 acres. Features fragrance garden, Mediterranean collection, and moon-viewing pavilion.
Location: San Francisco
Phone: (415) 661-1316

❾ MARINE WORLD AFRICA/USA

Famous oceanarium and 160-acre wildlife park has more than 1,000 animals. Highlights include themed shows, ecology theater, butterfly world, petting zoo, and elephant and camel rides. Ferry service is available from San Francisco.
Location: Vallejo
Phone: (707) 643-6722

❿ AUDUBON CANYON RANCH

Numerous trails wind through this 1,000-acre sanctuary encompassing redwood groves and a salt marsh. Features heron and egret nesting sites, a museum and bookstore.
Location: Stinson Beach
Phone: (415) 868-9244

CENTRAL VALLEY

NATURAL ATTRACTIONS & SANCTUARIES

Parks/Wildlife Areas

❶ SACRAMENTO NATIONAL WILDLIFE REFUGE
The single most important refuge on the Pacific flyway attracts more than two million migrating ducks and geese. Man-made marshes are intensely managed to provide an ideal wetland habitat. A birder's paradise throughout the year.
Location: Near Willows
Phone: (530) 934-2801

❷ GRAY LODGE WILDLIFE AREA
Over 6,500 acres of ponds attract more than 230 bird species and millions of migrating waterfowl. Bird populations peak October-January.
Location: North of Yuba City
Phone: (530) 846-7500

❸ TULE ELK STATE RESERVE
Reserve sustains four endangered species and herds of majestic tule elk. Marshes, ponds and grasslands support a wide diversity of plant and animal life. Guided tours are available.
Location: Near Bakersfield
Phone: (661) 764-6881

❹ KERN NATIONAL WILDLIFE REFUGE
Over 10,000 acres of marshes and grassland support an abundance of birds including waterfowl, shorebirds, herons and birds of prey.
Location: Delano
Phone: (661) 725-2767

❺ CASWELL MEMORIAL STATE PARK
Over 250 acres of virgin stands of huge oaks, willows and cottonwoods. Abundant birds and mammals.
Location: Near Modesto
Phone: (209) 599-3810

❻ LOS BANOS WILDLIFE AREA
3,200-acre grassland/wetland ecosystem supports a vast array of wildlife including more than 200 species of birds. This is one of many wildlife refuges in the Central Valley that is carefully managed in order to divert large bird populations from surrounding farm crops.
Location: Los Banos
Phone: (209) 826-0463

Museums/Sanctuaries

❼ CALIFORNIA LIVING MUSEUM
Botanical garden and zoo feature native plants and animals.
Location: Bakersfield
Phone: (661) 872-2256

❽ MERCER CAVERNS
Since 1885, people have come to marvel at ancient crystalline and rock formations in 10 caverns. Guided tours.
Location: Murphys
Phone: (209) 728-2101

❾ YOSEMITE WILDLIFE MUSEUM
Features impressive dioramas of North American wildlife.
Location: Merced
Phone: (209) 383-1052

❿ NIMBUS HATCHERIES
Migrating chinook salmon and steelhead can be seen in autumn and winter climbing the fish ladder below Nimbus Dam. Hatchery raises more than four million fry annually.
Location: Near Sacramento
Phone: (916) 358-2820

⓫ GREAT VALLEY MUSEUM OF NATURAL HISTORY
Highlights the natural history of the Central Valley and local plants and animals.
Location: Modesto
Phone: (209) 575-6196

SIERRA NEVADA

Tahoe City

5

7 South LakeTahoe

8

Arnold **4**

1 **6**

Bishop

3

2 Independence

Three Rivers

Parks/Wildlife Areas

The Sierra National Parks are world-renowned for their spectacular scenery and natural attractions.

❶ YOSEMITE NATIONAL PARK

California's first national park is arguably its most famous natural attraction. Located in the heart of the Sierra Nevada, it features spectacular waterfalls, groves of giant sequoias, huge alpine meadows, pinnacles, canyons, lakes and rivers. Two of its waterfalls are among the 10 highest on earth. Three visitor centers, four museums, tours, guided hikes, extensive interpretive programs and hotel and campground accommodations are available.

Location: Yosemite National Park
Phone: (209) 372-0200

❷ SEQUOIA AND KINGS CANYON NATIONAL PARKS

Adjacent parks in the southern Sierra feature thousands of acres of giant sequoias in a breathtaking alpine setting. Among the sequoias are the two largest trees (in mass) on earth. Highlights include Heather Lake, General Grant Grove, Mineral King sub-alpine meadows, Tharp's Log, Tunnel Log and Crystal Cave.

Location: Three Rivers
Phone: (559) 565-3341

❸ INYO NATIONAL FOREST

Includes 1,100 miles of trails and six wilderness areas. Main attractions are the Devil's Postpile National Monument, the Ancient Bristlecone Pine Forest (home to the oldest living trees on earth), Mono Basin National Forest Scenic Area, John Muir Wilderness (California's largest), Mammoth Lakes Resort Area, and Mount Whitney, the highest mountain in the lower 48 states.

Location: Bishop
Phone: (760) 647-3044

❹ CALAVERAS BIG TREES STATE PARK

6,000-acre park encompasses groves of giant sequoias. Visitor's center highlights local nature and history. 128 summer campsites are available.

Location: Arnold
Phone: (209) 795-2334

❺ DESOLATION WILDERNESS AREA

Popular wilderness destination has more than 50 lakes and 100 miles of trails. Encompasses over 63,000 acres of mountainous terrain.

Location: Near South Lake Tahoe
Phone: (530) 543-2600

❻ MONO LAKE TUFA STATE RESERVE

A sanctuary for one million migrating birds, the lake is more noted for the spire-like, calcium-carbonate tufas rising above the water and dotting the shoreline.

Location: Near Lee Vining
Phone: (760) 647-6331

❼ EMERALD BAY STATE PARK

Located on the southwest corner of Lake Tahoe – the world's largest alpine lake – it features some of the most photographed scenery in the area. The mountain vistas and remarkably clear, jewel-like waters are truly breathtaking.

Location: Near South Lake Tahoe
Phone: (530) 541-3030

Museums/Sanctuaries

❽ LAKE TAHOE VISITORS CENTER

Self-guided trails through marshes, forests and meadows provide insight into the local natural history. Underwater viewing tank offers visitors a glimpse of stream life including migrating trout (in season) and the occasional beaver.

Location: Near South Lake Tahoe
Phone: (530) 573-2600 - June-Sept.

CENTRAL COAST

Santa Cruz

Pacific Grove
Carmel
Monterey

Big Sur

Lucida

San Simeon

Morro Bay

San Luis Obispo

Pismo Beach
Santa Maria

Soledad

Solvang

Parks/Wildlife Areas

① JULIA PFEIFFER BURNS STATE PARK
3,500-acre park on the rugged Big Sur coastline encompasses some of the area's finest attractions including groves of redwoods, oaks and madrone, and a high waterfall that cascades into the ocean. Birds and marine mammals are abundant. The park's offshore area is an under-water reserve.
Location: Big Sur
Phone: (831) 667-2315

② AÑO NUEVO STATE RESERVE
A major gathering area for northern elephant seals and sea lions. Huge male elephant seals battle each other for females and territories during breeding season from December to March.
Location: North of Santa Cruz
Phone: (650) 879-0227

③ BIG BASIN REDWOODS STATE PARK
California's oldest state park features 18,000 acres of old growth redwoods, waterfalls and streams.
Location: North of Santa Cruz
Phone: (831) 338-8860

④ LAKE SAN ANTONIO
This huge lake is home to Southern California's largest population of wintering bald eagles and a herd of more than 400 deer. Excellent birding opportunities.
Location: South of King City
Phone: (805) 472-2311

⑤ GUADALUPE NIPOMO DUNES PRESERVE
California's most extensive coastal sand dunes include beach dunes over 500 ft. high (152 m). Abundant land and marine birds.
Location: South of Pismo Beach
Phone: (805) 343-2455

⑥ POINT LOBOS STATE RESERVE
550-acre reserve is noted for its populations of seabirds, sea lions, seals and sea otters and as a viewpoint for observing migrating whales.
Location: South of Carmel
Phone: (831) 624-4909

⑦ PINNACLES NATIONAL MONUMENT
Noted for its spire-like rock formations which are remnants of an ancient volcano.
Location: Near Soledad
Phone: (831) 389-4485

Museums/Sanctuaries

⑧ MONTEREY BAY AQUARIUM
A world-famous aquarium featuring more than 100 exhibits of Monterey Bay marine life. Highlights include bat ray petting pool, three-story kelp forest, sea otter tank, touch tide pool and aviary.
Location: Monterey
Phone: (831) 648-4888

⑨ PACIFIC GROVE MUSEUM OF NATURAL HISTORY
Changing exhibits highlight the natural history of Monterey County. Extensive bird and rock collections.
Location: Pacific Grove
Phone: (831) 648-5716

⑩ MORRO BAY STATE PARK MUSEUM OF NATURAL HISTORY
Exhibits highlight local habitats, ecology, marine life, geology and Native American history.
Location: Morro Bay
Phone: (805) 772-2694

⑪ SANTA CRUZ MUSEUM OF NATURAL HISTORY
Features numerous displays on fossils, regional plants and animals, and local natural history.
Location: Santa Cruz
Phone: (831) 420-6115

SOUTH COAST

Santa Barbara
Ventura
Los Angeles
Long Beach
San Clemente
San Bernardino
Escondido
San Diego

Parks/Wildlife Areas

❶ CHANNEL ISLANDS NATIONAL PARK

A naturalist's paradise, this unique sanctuary encompasses five islands featuring sea stacks, caves, abundant marine animals and sea birds. Boat and plane expeditions depart from Ventura.
Location: Ventura
Phone: (805) 658-5730

❷ ANGELES NATIONAL FOREST

Mountainous preserve encompasses habitats ranging from alpine meadows to deserts. 80 campgrounds and six ski resorts are found within the park boundaries.
Location: North of Arcadia
Phone: (626) 574-1613

❸ SANTA MONICA MOUNTAINS NATIONAL RECREATION AREA

Beaches, rugged mountains and rolling wooded hills are a popular biking and hiking destination. Interpretive programs and guided hikes are offered throughout the year.
Location: Near Los Angeles
Phone: (805) 370-2301

Museums/Sanctuaries

❹ NATURAL HISTORY MUSEUM OF LOS ANGELES COUNTY

Outstanding exhibits on African and American animal habitats, local plants and animals, dinosaurs and geology.
Location: Los Angeles
Phone: (213) 763-3466

❺ GEORGE C. PAGE MUSEUM OF LA BREA DISCOVERIES

Highlights fossils of 200 varieties of plants and animals (including humans) from the million fossils extracted from the adjacent La Brea Tar Pits. Life-size skeletons of sabre-toothed cats and mammoths are among the attractions.
Location: Los Angeles
Phone: (323) 934-7243

❻ LOS ANGELES & BOTANIC GARDEN COUNTY ARBORETUM

Over 125 acres of local and exotic trees and shrubs. Includes a bird sanctuary and horticultural research center.
Location: Arcadia
Phone: (626) 821-3222

❼ HUNTINGTON LIBRARY, ART COLLECTIONS, AND BOTANICAL GARDENS

207-acre estate features 14,000 plants from around the world including rare shrubs and trees. Attractions include a rose garden, Japanese garden, Zen rock garden and desert garden. Tours available.
Location: San Marino
Phone: (626) 405-2100

❽ SAN DIEGO ZOO

One of the world's largest and best zoos, it houses 3,400 animals in an 100-acre botanical garden. World-renowned for its exotic and rare species including Chinese pandas.
Location: San Diego
Phone: (619) 234-3153

❾ SEA WORLD

150-acre marine park features a killer whale stadium, avian exhibit, touch tidepool and the world's largest collection of sharks.
Location: San Diego
Phone: (619) 226-3901

❿ SANTA BARBARA MUSEUM OF NATURAL HISTORY

Exhibits highlight local plants, animals, geology, ecology, fossils, marine life, Native American history and the Channel Islands.
Location: Santa Barbara
Phone: (805) 682-4711

DESERT

Death Valley Jct.

Mojave

Barstow

6

Ludlow

Needles

5

8 Palm Springs

Parker

9 7 3

4

Borrego Springs

2

Boulevard

Parks/Wildlife Areas

DEATH VALLEY NATIONAL PARK

Once the floor of an inland sea, Death Valley is a veritable moonscape with sand dunes, salt flats and volcanic craters. Highlights include Dante's View at 5,474 ft. (1,670 m) above sea level, Badwater at 282 ft. (86 m) below sea level (the lowest point in the U.S.) and ghost town ruins. Abundant desert mammals and reptiles.
Location: Death Valley
Phone: (760) 786-3200

ANZA-BORREGO DESERT STATE PARK

California's largest state park protects over 600,000 acres of badlands, washes, woodlands and mile-high mountains. Abundant wildlife includes more than 60 mammals, 220 birds and 60 reptiles and amphibians.
Location: Near Borrego Springs
Phone: (760) 767-5311

JOSHUA TREE NATIONAL PARK

High desert area with groves of Joshua trees, giant yuccas, spring wildflowers, palm trees, birds and desert bighorn sheep. Guided walks and hikes in the spring and fall.
Location: Twentynine Palms
Phone: (760) 367-5500

SALTON SEA NATIONAL WILDLIFE REFUGE

One of the world's largest inland seas was created in 1905 when the Colorado River broke through a dike and flooded a saline lake bed for two years. This 37,000-acre refuge of fresh- and saltwater habitats is home to a diverse array of plant and animal life. Nearly 400 bird species have been recorded here.
Location: Northwest of Calipatria
Phone: (760) 348-5278

❺ MOUNT SAN JACINTO STATE PARK

Wilderness area encompasses three craggy peaks over 10,000 ft. high (3,048 m). Alpine forests and meadows can be viewed from an aerial tram that takes passengers 2.5 miles up the mountain.
Location: Palm Springs
Phone: (951) 659-2607

❻ PROVIDENCE MOUNTAINS STATE RECREATION AREA

Scenic park features huge limestone caverns and a large resident bat population. Over 140 bird species and 35 reptiles and amphibians are found here.
Location: East of Barstow
Phone: (760) 928-2586

Museums/Sanctuaries

❼ THE LIVING DESERT

1,200-acre wildlife park and botanical garden celebrates the beauty and diversity of desert life. Features hundreds of species of exotic desert plants, an aviary, coyote grotto and bighorn sheep habitat. Self-guided trails.
Location: Palm Desert
Phone: (760) 346-5694

❽ MOORTEN'S BOTANICAL GARDEN

Self-guided trails wind through 2,000 species of desert plants. Also features a wildlife feeding area.
Location: Palm Springs
Phone: (760) 327-6555

❾ PALM SPRINGS DESERT MUSEUM

Dioramas and exhibits highlight local natural history, science and western art.
Location: Palm Springs
Phone: (760) 325-0189

MAMMALS

- ❏ American Badger
- ❏ American Beaver
- ❏ Bighorn Sheep
- ❏ Black Bear
- ❏ Black Rat
- ❏ Black-tailed Jackrabbit
- ❏ Bobcat
- ❏ Brazilian Free-tailed Bat
- ❏ Brush Rabbit
- ❏ California Ground Squirrel
- ❏ California Mole
- ❏ California Myotis
- ❏ California Sea Lion
- ❏ California Vole
- ❏ Common Dolphin
- ❏ Common Gray Fox
- ❏ Common Porcupine
- ❏ Common Raccoon
- ❏ Coyote
- ❏ Dall's Porpoise
- ❏ Deer Mouse
- ❏ Desert Cottontail
- ❏ Dusky-footed Woodrat
- ❏ Elk
- ❏ Finback Whale
- ❏ Golden-mantled Ground Squirrel
- ❏ Gray Whale
- ❏ Harbor Seal
- ❏ House Mouse
- ❏ Humpback Whale
- ❏ Killer Whale
- ❏ Long-tailed Weasel
- ❏ Merriam's Chipmunk
- ❏ Mink
- ❏ Mountain Lion
- ❏ Mule Deer
- ❏ Northern Elephant Seal
- ❏ Northern Flying Squirrel
- ❏ Northern River Otter
- ❏ Norway Rat
- ❏ Ornate Shrew
- ❏ Pacific White-sided Dolphin
- ❏ Ringtail
- ❏ Sea Otter
- ❏ Striped Skunk
- ❏ Virginia Opossum
- ❏ Western Gray Squirrel
- ❏ Western Jumping Mouse
- ❏ Western Red Bat
- ❏ Western Spotted Skunk
- ❏ Yellow-bellied Marmot

BIRDS

- ❏ Acorn Woodpecker
- ❏ American Avocet
- ❏ American Coot
- ❏ American Goldfinch
- ❏ American Kestrel
- ❏ American Robin
- ❏ American Wigeon
- ❏ Anna's Hummingbird
- ❏ Ash-throated Flycatcher
- ❏ Bald Eagle
- ❏ Belted Kingfisher
- ❏ Black Oystercatcher
- ❏ Black-crowned Night-Heron
- ❏ Black-necked Stilt
- ❏ Blue-winged Teal
- ❏ Brown Pelican
- ❏ Brown-headed Cowbird
- ❏ Bullock's Oriole
- ❏ California Condor
- ❏ California Gull
- ❏ California Quail
- ❏ California Thrasher
- ❏ Canada Goose
- ❏ Cedar Waxwing
- ❏ Chestnut-backed Chickadee
- ❏ Chipping Sparrow
- ❏ Cinnamon Teal
- ❏ Clark's Nutcracker
- ❏ Common Crow
- ❏ Common Merganser
- ❏ Common Nighthawk
- ❏ Common Raven
- ❏ Common Snipe
- ❏ Common Yellowthroat
- ❏ Dark-eyed Junco
- ❏ Double-crested Cormorant
- ❏ Downy Woodpecker
- ❏ European Starling
- ❏ Golden Eagle
- ❏ Great Blue Heron
- ❏ Great Egret
- ❏ Greater Roadrunner
- ❏ Great Horned Owl
- ❏ Green Heron
- ❏ Green-winged Teal
- ❏ Hairy Woodpecker
- ❏ Horned Lark

❏ House Finch
❏ House Sparrow
❏ House Wren
❏ Killdeer
❏ Lazuli Bunting
❏ Least Sandpiper
❏ Long-billed Curlew
❏ Mallard
❏ Marbled Godwit
❏ Marsh Wren
❏ Mourning Dove
❏ Northern Flicker
❏ Northern Harrier
❏ Northern Mockingbird
❏ Northern Pintail
❏ Northern Shoveler
❏ Oak Titmouse
❏ Orange-crowned Warbler
❏ Osprey
❏ Pied-billed Grebe
❏ Pine Siskin
❏ Red-tailed Hawk
❏ Red-winged Blackbird
❏ Ring-billed Gull
❏ Ring-necked Pheasant
❏ Rock Pigeon
❏ Ruddy Duck
❏ Sanderling
❏ Snow Goose
❏ Snowy Egret
❏ Song Sparrow
❏ Spotted Sandpiper
❏ Spotted Towhee
❏ Steller's Jay
❏ Surf Scoter
❏ Turkey Vulture
❏ Violet-green Swallow
❏ Western Bluebird
❏ Western Grebe
❏ Western Gull
❏ Western Meadowlark
❏ Western Scrub-Jay
❏ Western Tanager
❏ White-breasted Nuthatch
❏ Willet
❏ Wood Duck
❏ Yellow Warbler
❏ Yellow-billed Magpie
❏ Yellow-headed Blackbird
❏ Yellow-rumped Warbler

REPTILES

❏ California Red-sided Garter Snake
❏ California Whiptail
❏ Collared Lizard
❏ Common Kingsnake
❏ Desert Tortoise
❏ Monterey Ringneck Snake
❏ Pacific Gopher Snake
❏ Red-eared Slider
❏ Side-blotched Lizard
❏ Southern Alligator Lizard
❏ Western Aquatic Garter Snake
❏ Western Banded Gecko
❏ Western Fence Lizard
❏ Western Pond Turtle
❏ Western Rattlesnake
❏ Western Yellowbelly Racer
❏ Pacific Gopher Snake

AMPHIBIANS

❏ Bullfrog
❏ California Newt
❏ California Slender Salamander
❏ California Tiger Salamander
❏ California Toad
❏ Northern Leopard Frog
❏ Northwestern Salamander
❏ Pacific Giant Salamander
❏ Pacific Treefrog
❏ Red-legged Frog
❏ Western Spadefoot Toad

FISHES

❏ Albacore
❏ Bat Ray
❏ Black Crappie
❏ Black-and-yellow Rockfish
❏ Bluegill
❏ Brook Trout
❏ Brown Trout
❏ California Barracuda
❏ California Halibut
❏ California Roach
❏ California Sheephead
❏ Chinook (King) Salmon
❏ Chum (Dog) Salmon
❏ Coho (Silver) Salmon

SPECIES CHECKLIST

- ❏ Common Carp
- ❏ Garibaldi
- ❏ Golden Shiner
- ❏ Golden Trout
- ❏ Goldfish
- ❏ Largemouth Bass
- ❏ Leopard Shark
- ❏ Lingcod
- ❏ Mosquitofish
- ❏ Northern Anchovy
- ❏ Pacific Bonito
- ❏ Pacific Hake
- ❏ Pacific Herring
- ❏ Pacific Lamprey
- ❏ Pacific Mackerel
- ❏ Rainbow Trout
- ❏ Sacramento Sucker
- ❏ Smallmouth Bass
- ❏ Sockeye (Red) Salmon
- ❏ Speckled Dace
- ❏ Spiny Dogfish
- ❏ Starry Flounder
- ❏ Steelhead Trout
- ❏ Striped Bass
- ❏ Striped Seaperch
- ❏ Threespine Stickleback
- ❏ Vermilion Rockfish
- ❏ White Crappie
- ❏ White Sturgeon
- ❏ Yellowtail

SEASHORE LIFE

- ❏ Acorn Barnacle
- ❏ Black Abalone
- ❏ Black Turban Snail
- ❏ Blue Mussel
- ❏ Brooding Anemone
- ❏ Bull Kelp
- ❏ California Horn Snail
- ❏ California Mussel
- ❏ Dungeness Crab
- ❏ Eelgrass
- ❏ Giant Green Anemone
- ❏ Giant Pacific Oyster
- ❏ Giant Spined Sea Star
- ❏ Hermit Crab
- ❏ Moon Jellyfish
- ❏ Native Littleneck Clam
- ❏ Ochre Sea Star
- ❏ Pacific Pink Scallop
- ❏ Purple Sea Urchin
- ❏ Purple Shore Crab
- ❏ Red Crab
- ❏ Rockweed
- ❏ Rough Keyhole Limpet
- ❏ Sail Jellyfish
- ❏ Sand Dollar
- ❏ Sea Palm

TREES & SHRUBS

- ❏ Arroyo Willow
- ❏ Bigleaf Maple
- ❏ Bitter Cherry
- ❏ Blueblossom
- ❏ Bristlecone Pine
- ❏ California Black Oak
- ❏ California Buckeye
- ❏ California Fan Palm
- ❏ California Juniper
- ❏ California Laurel
- ❏ California Live Oak
- ❏ California Scrub Oak
- ❏ California Sycamore
- ❏ California Torreya
- ❏ California White Oak
- ❏ Canary Palm
- ❏ Chamise
- ❏ Coconut Palm
- ❏ Common Manzanita
- ❏ Coyote Brush
- ❏ Creosote Bush
- ❏ Date Palm
- ❏ Douglas-fir
- ❏ European White Birch
- ❏ Fremont Cottonwood
- ❏ Giant Sequoia
- ❏ Honey Mesquite
- ❏ Incense-cedar
- ❏ Joshua-tree
- ❏ Jumping Cholla
- ❏ Lodgepole Pine
- ❏ Lombardy Poplar
- ❏ Mohave Yucca
- ❏ Monterey Cypress
- ❏ Mountain Mahogany
- ❏ Pacific Madrone
- ❏ Pacific Yew
- ❏ Ponderosa Pine
- ❏ Redwood
- ❏ Singleleaf Pinyon Pine
- ❏ Sugar Pine
- ❏ Teddybear Cholla
- ❏ Toyon

❏ Trembling Aspen
❏ Weeping Willow
❏ Western Red Cedar
❏ Western White Pine
❏ White Alder
❏ White Fir

WILDFLOWERS

White
❏ Arrowhead
❏ Beach Strawberry
❏ Bindweed
❏ Common Ice Plant
❏ Cow Parsnip
❏ Desert Lily
❏ Elegant Camas
❏ English Daisy
❏ Fragrant Waterlily
❏ Indian Pipe
❏ Our Lord's Candle
❏ Pacific Dogwood
❏ Phlox
❏ Poison Oak
❏ Southwestern Thornapple
❏ White Clover
❏ White Sweet Clover
❏ White Trillium
❏ White Virgin's-Bower
❏ Yarrow

Yellow, Orange & Green
❏ Barrel Cactus
❏ Blazing Star
❏ California Poppy
❏ Common Cattail
❏ Common Dandelion
❏ Common Monkey Flower
❏ Common Plantain
❏ Common Sunflower
❏ Creamcups
❏ Desert Candle
❏ Desert Prickly Pear Cactus
❏ Evening Primrose
❏ Goldenrod
❏ Goldfields
❏ Great Basin Sagebrush
❏ Rabbitbrush
❏ Redwood Violet
❏ Shrubby Cinquefoil
❏ Stinging Nettle
❏ St. John's Wort

❏ Subalpine Buttercup
❏ Tarweed
❏ Tree Tabacco
❏ Woolly Mullein
❏ Yellow Salsify
❏ Yellow Sand Verbena

Red & Pink
❏ Beavertail Cactus
❏ Bitterroot
❏ California Fuschia
❏ California Rhododendron
❏ Canada Thistle
❏ Cardinal Flower
❏ Common Fleabane
❏ Desert Globemallow
❏ Farewell-to-Spring
❏ Fireweed
❏ Foxglove
❏ Fringe Cups
❏ Indian Paintbrush
❏ Pine Drops
❏ Pipsissewa
❏ Red Columbine
❏ Redwood Sorrel
❏ Shooting Star
❏ Skyrocket
❏ Striped Coral Root
❏ Twinflower
❏ Wild Ginger
❏ Woods' Rose

Blue & Purple
❏ American Vetch
❏ Aster
❏ Baby Blue Eyes
❏ Bluebells
❏ Blue-eyed Grass
❏ Chicory
❏ Common Camas
❏ Desert Sand Verbena
❏ Elegant Brodiaea
❏ Fringed Gentian
❏ Miniature Lupine
❏ Mission Bells
❏ Monkshood
❏ Oysterplant
❏ Purple Loosestrife
❏ Showy Milkweed
❏ Wild Blue Flax
❏ Wild Teasel

Alternate
Spaced singly along the stem.

Anther
The part of the stamen that produces pollen.

Anadromous
Living in saltwater, breeding in freshwater.

Annual
A plant which completes its life cycle in one year.

Anterior
Pertaining to the front end.

Aquatic
Living in water.

Aquifer
Underground chamber or layer of rock that holds water.

Ascending
Rising or curving upward.

Barbel
An organ near the mouth of fish used to taste, touch, or smell.

Barrier Island
Sandbar off the mainland that protects the coast from wave action.

Berry
A fruit formed from a single ovary which is fleshy or pulpy and contains one or many seeds.

Bloom
A whitish powdery or waxy covering.

Brackish
Water that is part freshwater and part saltwater.

Bract
A modified – often scale-like – leaf, usually small.

Branchlet
A twig from which leaves grow.

Boss
A rounded knob between the eyes of some toads.

Burrow
A tunnel excavated and inhabited by an animal.

Carnivorous
Feeding primarily on meat.

Catkin
A caterpillar-like drooping cluster of small flowers.

Cold-blooded
Refers to animals which are unable to regulate their own body temperature. 'Ectotherm' is the preferred term for this characteristic since many 'cold-blooded' species like reptiles are at times able to maintain a warmer body temperature than that of 'warm-blooded' species like mammals.

Conifer
A cone-bearing tree, usually evergreen.

Coral
The limestone skeletal deposits of coral polyps.

Coverts
Small feathers that cover the underside (undertail) or top (uppertail) of the base of bird's tail.

Deciduous
Shedding leaves annually.

Dicots
Plants with two embryonic leaves at germination, net-veined leaves, stems with cylindrical vascular bundles in a regular pattern that contain cambium.

Diurnal
Active primarily during the day.

Dorsal
Pertaining to the back or upper surface.

Ecology
The study of the relationships between organisms, and between organisms and their environment.

Endangered
Species threatened with extinction.

Epiphyte
A plant that obtains nourishment from nutrients in the air and rain. They often live on host plants like trees without harming them.

Endemic
Living only in a particular area.

Flower
Reproductive structure of a plant.

Flower stalk
The stem bearing the flowers.

Fruit
The matured, seed-bearing ovary.

Gamete
An egg or sperm cell.

Habitat
The physical area in which organisms live.

Herbivorous
Feeding primarily on vegetation.

Insectivorous
Feeding primarily on insects.

Introduced
Species brought by humans to an area outside its normal range.

Invertebrate
Animals lacking backbones, e.g., worms, slugs, crustaceans, insects, shellfish.

Larva
Immature forms of an animal which differ from the adult.

Lateral
Located away from the mid-line, at or near the sides.

Lobe
A projecting part of a leaf or flower, usually rounded.

Molting
Loss of feathers, hair or skin while renewing plumage, coat or scales.

Monocots
Plants with one embryonic leaf at germination, parallel-veined leaves, stems with scattered vascular bundles with little or no cambium.

Morphs
A color variation of a species that is regular and not related to sex, age or season.

Nest
A structure built for shelter or insulation.

Nocturnal
Active primarily at night.

Omnivorous
Feeding on both animal and vegetable food.

Ovary
The female sex organ which is the site of egg production and maturation.

Perennial
A plant that lives for several years.

Petal
The colored outer parts of a flower head.

Phase
Coloration other than typical.

Pistil
The central organ of the flower which develops into a fruit.

Pollen
The tiny grains produced in the anthers which contain the male reproductive cells.

Posterior
Pertaining to the rear.

Sepal
The outer, usually green, leaf-like structures that protect the flower bud and are located at the base of an open flower.

Species
A group of interbreeding organisms which are reproductively isolated from other groups.

Speculum
A brightly colored, iridescent patch on the wings of some birds, especially ducks.

Spur
A pointed projection.

Subspecies
A relatively uniform, distinct portion of a species population.

Threatened
Species not yet endangered but in imminent danger of being so.

Ungulate
An animal that has hooves.

Ventral
Pertaining to the under or lower surface.

Vertebrate
An animal possessing a backbone.

Warm-blooded
An animal which regulates its blood temperature internally. 'Endotherm' is the preferred term for this characteristic.

Whorl
A circle of leaves or flowers about a stem.

Woolly
Bearing long or matted hairs.

BIBLIOGRAPHY

MAMMALS

Boitani, Luigi and Stefania Bartoli. *Simon & Schuster's Guide to Mammals.* New York: Simon & Schuster, 1983.
Burt, William Henry. *A Field Guide to the Mammals: Field Marks of All North American Species Found North of Mexico.* 3rd ed. Boston: Houghton Mifflin, 1976.
Carwardine, Mark. *Eyewitness Handbooks: Whales, Dolphins and Porpoises.* New York: Dorling Kindersley, 1995.
Ingles, Lloyd, G. *Mammals of the Pacific States.* Stanford: Stanford University Press, 1965.
Murie, Olaus J. *A Field Guide to Animal Tracks.* 2nd ed. Boston: Houghton Mifflin, 1982.
Walker, Ernest P., et al. *Mammals of the World.* 2 vols. Baltimore: Johns Hopkins Press, 1965.
Whitaker, John O., Jr. *National Audubon Society Field Guide to North American Mammals.* Rev. ed. New York: Alfred A. Knopf, 1996.
Wilson, Don E. and Sue Ruff, eds. *The Smithsonian Book of North American Mammals.* Washington, D.C.: Smithsonian Institution Press, 1999.

BIRDS

Alsop, Fred J., III. *Smithsonian Handbooks Birds of North America: Western Region.* New York: Dorling Kindersley, 2001.
Barnard, Edward S. and Sharon Fass Yates, eds. *Reader's Digest North American Wildlife: Birds.* Pleasantville: Reader's Digest Association, 1998.
Clark, Herbert. *Natural History of the White-Inyo Range.* Berkeley: University of California Press, 1991.
Cogswell, H.L. *Water Birds of California.* Berkeley: University of California Press, 1977.
Latimer, Jonathan P., et al. *Birds of North America: A Guide to Field Identification.* Rev. and updated. New York: St. Martin's Press, 2001.
National Geographic Field Guide to the Birds of North America. 4th ed. Washington, D.C.: National Geographic Society, 1987.
Peterson, Roger Tory. *A Field Guide to Western Birds.* 3rd ed. Boston: Houghton Mifflin, 1990.
Sibley, David Allen. *The Sibley Guide to Birds.* New York: Alfred A. Knopf, 2000.
Small, Arnold. *The Birds of California.* New York: Winchester Press, 1974.
Udvardy, Miklos D.F. *The Audubon Society Field Guide to North American Birds: Western Region.* New York: Alfred A. Knopf, 1994.

REPTILES & AMPHIBIANS

Behler, John L. *National Audubon Society Field Guide to North American Reptiles and Amphibians.* New York: Alfred A. Knopf, 1979.
Behler, John L. *National Audubon Society Pocket Guide: Familiar Reptiles and Amphibians of North America.* New York: Alfred A. Knopf, 1995.
Capula, Massimo. *Simon & Schuster's Guide to Reptiles and Amphibians of the World.* New York: Simon & Schuster, 1989.
Conant, Roger and Joseph T. Collins. *A Field Guide to Reptiles and Amphibians: Eastern and Central North America.* 3rd ed. Boston: Houghton Mifflin, 1998.
Smith, Hobart M. and Edmund D. Brodie, Jr. *Reptiles of North America: A Guide to Field Identification.* New York: St. Martin's Press, 1982.
Stebbins, Robert C. *A Field Guide to Western Reptiles and Amphibians.* 2nd ed. Boston: Houghton Mifflin, 1985.
Stebbins, Robert C. *Amphibians and Reptiles of California.* Berkeley: University of California Press, 1972.
Ubertazzi Tanara, Milli. *The World of Amphibians and Reptiles.* Berkshire: Sampson Low, 1978.
Zim, Herbert S. and Hobart M. Smith. *Reptiles and Amphibians.* Rev. ed. New York: Golden Press, 1987.

FISHES

Boschung, Herbert T. Jr., et al. *National Audubon Society Field Guide to North American Fishes, Whales, and Dolphins.* New York: Alfred A. Knopf, 1989.
Eschemeyer, William N. and Earl S. Herald. *A Field Guide to Pacific Coast Fishes.* Boston: Houghton Mifflin, 1983.
Gilbert, Carter R. and James D. Williams. *National Audubon Society Field Guide to Fishes: North America.* Rev. ed. New York: Alfred A. Knopf, 2002.
Goodson, Gar. *Fishes of the Pacific Coast.* Stanford: Stanford University Press, 1996.
Moyler, P.B. *Inland Fishes of California.* Berkeley: University of California Press, 1976.
Page, Lawrence and Brooks M. Burr. *A Field Guide to Freshwater Fishes: North America North of Mexico.* Boston: Houghton Mifflin, 1991.
Waller, Geoffrey, ed. *SeaLife: A Complete Guide to the Marine Environment.* Washington, D.C.: Smithsonian Institution Press, 1996.

SEASHORE LIFE

Abbott, R. Tucker. *Seashells of North America: A Guide to Field Identification.* New York: Golden Press, 1968.

Dawson, E.Y. and M.S. Foster. *Seashore Plants of California.* Berkeley: University of California Press, 1982.

Hinton, Sam. *Seashore Life of California.* Berkeley: University of California Press, 1987.

Meinkoth, Norman A. *National Audubon Society Field Guide to North American Seashore Creatures.* New York: Alfred A. Knopf, 1998.

Miller, Arthur P., Jr., and Marjorie L. Miller. *Park Ranger Guide to Seashores.* Harrisburg: Stackpole Books, 1992.

Rehder, Harald A. *The Audubon Society Guide to North American Seashells.* New York: Alfred A. Knopf, 2000.

FLORA

Barnard, Edward S. and Sharon Fass Yates, eds. *Reader's Digest North American Wildlife: Wildflowers.* Pleasantville: Reader's Digest Association, 1998.

Brockman, C.F. *Trees of North America.* New York: Golden Press, 1979.

Coombes, Allen J. *Eye Witness Handbooks: Trees.* New York: Dorling Kindersley, 1992.

Elias, Thomas S. *The Complete Trees of North America: Field Guide and Natural History.* New York: Van Nostrand Reinhold, 1980.

Kricher, John C. *A Field Guide to the Ecology of Western Forests.* Boston: Houghton Mifflin, 1993.

Lanzara, Paoloa and Mariella Pizzetti. *Simon & Schuster's Guide to Trees.* New York: Simon & Schuster, 1978.

Little, Elbert L. *National Audubon Society Field Guide to North American Trees:* Western Region. New York: Alfred A. Knopf, 1980.

Munz, P.A. *A Flora of Southern California.* Berkeley: University of California Press, 1974.

Ornduff, Robert. *An Introduction to California Plant Life.* Berkeley: University of California Press, 1974.

Petrides, George A. *A Field Guide to Western Trees: Western United States and Canada.* Boston: Houghton Mifflin, 1998.

Spellenberg, Richard. *National Audubon Society Field Guide to North American Wildflowers: Western Region.* Rev. ed. New York: Alfred A. Knopf, 2001.

Venning, Frank D. *Wildflowers of North America: A Guide to Field Identification.* New York: Golden Press, 1984.

NATURAL HISTORY

Alden, Peter, et al. *National Audubon Society Field Guide to California.* New York: Alfred A. Knopf, 1998.

Benyus, Janine M. *The Field Guide to Wildlife Habitats of the Western United States.* New York: Simon & Schuster, 1989.

Henson, P. and Ussner, D.J. *The Natural History of Big Sur.* Berkeley: University of California Press, 1994.

McConnaughey, Bayard H. and Evelyn McConnaughey. *Pacific Coast.* New York: Alfred A. Knopf, 1994.

McNab, W. Henry and Peter E. Avers. *Ecological Subregions of the United States: Section Descriptions.* Washington, D.C.: United States Department of Agriculture, 1994.

McQueen, Jane B, ed. *The Complete Guide to America's National Parks.* 1994-1995 ed. Washington, D.C.: National Park Foundation, 1995.

Perry, J. and J.G. Perry. *The Sierra Club Guide to the Natural Areas of California.* San Francisco: Sierra Club Books, 1983.

Ransom, Jay Ellis. *Harper & Row's Complete Field Guide to North American Wildlife.* Western ed. New York: Harper & Row, 1981.

Riley, Laura and William Riley. *Guide to the National Wildlife Refuges.* New York: Collier Books, 1992.

Schoenherr, A.A. *A Natural History of California.* Berkeley: University of California Press, 1992.

Wernert, Susan J., ed. *Reader's Digest North American Wildlife.* Pleasantville: Reader's Digest Association, 1982.

Williams, J.C. and H.C. Monroe. *Natural History of Northern California.* Dubuque: Kendall/Hunt Publishing, 1976.

Vessel, M.P. and H.H. Wong. *The Natural History of Vacant Lots.* Berkeley: University of California Press, 1987.

INDEX

300 TITLES + 50 STATES = 3 MILLION SOLD

Waterford Press also produces simplified, pocket reference guides that introduce novices to travel, languages, science and nature. Laminated for durability, these handy folding guides are a great source of portable information – and are ready to take anywhere!

POCKET NATURALIST® GUIDES

Over 200 national, regional, state and city-specific titles to nature and natural phenomema, including a bird guide to every state!

- Animal Tracks
- The Night Sky
- Bugs & Slugs
- Butterflies & Moths
- Geology
- Weather
- Backyard Birds
- Mushrooms
- Dangerous Animals & Plants
- Edible Wild Plants
- Eastern Backyard Birds
- Trees
- Rocky Mountain Birds
- Dragonflies & Damselflies
- Arizona Birds
- Alaska Wildlife
- Texas Trees & Wildflowers
- Florida Birds
- Oregon Trees & Wildflowers
- Chicago Birds
- Los Angeles Birds
- Seattle Birds

POCKET TRAVELLER® GUIDES

Pocket-sized reference guides introduce novices to languages, the world's greatest cities and most prominent eco-tourism destinations.

- Instant French
- Instant Spanish
- Instant German
- Instant Italian
- London
- Paris
- Rome
- Galapagos Wildlife
- African Wildlife
- African Birds
- Australian Wildlife
- Australian Birds
- Caribbean Birds
- Costa Rican Wildlife
- Birds of Britain
- Field Guide to the Grand Canyon
- Denali National Park
- Yellowstone Wildlife
- Appalachian Trail Wildlife
- The Southern Night Sky

POCKET TUTOR® GUIDES

Pocket-sized reference guides provide quick pocket reference to a wide variety of topics.

- Cats
- Cattle & Horses
- Knots
- Dinosaurs
- Dogs
- House & Garden Pests
- Emergency First Aid
- Invasive Plants
- Medicinal Plants
- State Flags & Facts
- Wilderness Survival
- World Flags

For a catalog, or to order, call 800-434-2555 or visit our website at www.waterfordpress.com